Do This

COMMUNION FOR JUST AND COURAGEOUS LIVING

Do This

COMMUNION FOR JUST AND COURAGEOUS LIVING

EDITED BY
Mary Luti

God Is Still Speaking,®: The Writers' Group is composed of United Church of Christ ministers and writers who collaborate on resources for people in the church, outside the church, and not sure about the church. The Writers' Group and affiliated contributors are known for their whimsical piety, providing honest inspiration and progressive theological reflection for Christians who strive to be literate but not literal in nurturing their faith.

The Pilgrim Press
1300 East 9th Street, Suite 1100
Cleveland, OH 44122
thepilgrimpress.com

Published 2023.

Printed on acid-free paper.

Library of Congress Cataloging-in-Publication Data on file.
LCCN: 2023934956

ISBN 978-0-8298-0054-8 (paper)

Printed in The United States of America.

CONTENTS

BEARING FRUIT
Communion, Creation and Labor

ONE SKIN, ONE KIN
Communion and Bodies

NO ONE UNSATISFIED
Communion and Hunger

YOU GIVE THEM SOMETHING TO EAT

Communion and Just Mercy

EATING OUR WAY TO LOVE

Communion and Reconciliation

PLEASE, COME IN

Communion, Hospitality and Healing

FOR AS LONG AS IT TAKES

Communion and Perseverance

INDEXES

Introduction

On the night he was betrayed, Jesus ate supper with his friends. He gave God thanks for bread and wine and mysteriously called them his Body and Blood. Giving them to his disciples to eat and drink, he said, "Do this." And ever since, the church has gratefully obeyed, remembering Jesus by giving thanks, sharing a loaf and a cup, and experiencing a real and loving presence, just as he promised we would. Communion occupies a central place in Christian life. Although we often can't fully express what it means to us, we know enough that we've come to call it "holy."

Holy as it is, however, the way we think about and practice Communion has sometimes thinned out its thick meanings and toned down its bracing challenges. Communion packs an ethical wallop, but sometimes it's hard to feel it at our tables. For example, Communion is about unity, wholeness and welcome, but for many people it's also a painful occasion of judgment and exclusion. We call it a heavenly banquet, but we often betray that lavish generosity by serving only demure bits of bread and polite sips of juice. It's about Body and Blood, but we sometimes get so spiritual about Communion that we don't notice its implications for real human bodies, especially the violence we perpetrate on them. We cherish God's intimate nearness in Communion, but unbalanced by other considerations, that intimacy leads to a privatization of the sacrament, obscuring its crucial public witness.

From the earliest days of the Church, Communion was understood not only as a ritual by which Christ becomes truly present and strengthens our ties of Christian love, but also as a practice that produces just and courageous lives. By the power of the Spirit, participation in the sacrament is meant to shape us collectively into a body that behaves in a distinctive way in the world: a body that looks, sounds, thinks, speaks, and acts like Communion, doing in the world what we do at our tables whenever we "do this."

This is not to politicize Communion. It's to say that Communion is concerned with the ethics of our shared life and always has been. We invite you to reflect with us on some of these life-shaping dimensions of Communion—belonging, memory, bodies, violence, feeding, reconciliation, healing, creation care, resilience, human labor—and encourage you to incorporate them in your congregational practice of Communion.

It's a safe bet that some pieces in this resource will not fit your particular theology or your congregational context. Some may seem old hat. Others may open new perspectives. Some may go too far for you. Some not far enough. That's okay. Consider this resource a starting point, a nudge for further reflection, prayer, and practice. Perhaps it will help you live into the sacrament more deeply and be more open to the Spirit's work of transforming the church—Communion by Communion—into a table of love and justice in the world.

Suggestions for Use

Christian traditions across time and around the world have shaped diverse practices of Communion. Christians differ in the frequency with which we celebrate the sacrament. Some of our celebrations are solemn and formal, some informal and more joyous. We don't even agree on what to call the ritual: the Lord's Supper, Eucharist, Holy Mysteries, Communion. Orders of worship look different, too, with different titles for different portions of the Communion liturgy. Likewise, the use and placement of hymns throughout Communion varies among traditions.

In this resource, the diversity of writers' experiences of the order of Communion has been retained intentionally, as is evident in the varied section headings of liturgies. Feel free to adapt the headings as appropriate to a particular worship context, whether to maintain a "flow" that is expected by a congregation or to intentionally disrupt that flow. In some instances, the liturgies in this resource do not represent a full order of Communion but only part, allowing room for creativity in interweaving the new with the familiar. Bring thoughtfulness and wonder to the order of Communion, with the intention of creating an atmosphere in which the Christian body can be shaped by the Spirit as it is fed.

Section headings of the liturgies are identified by small caps. Bolded text is used to indicate "all voices," and unbolded text is used to indicate "singular voice/leader."

Additional ideas for using this resource:

The Reflections

- as personal or small group devotions
- as "sermon seeds," sermon illustrations for Communion Sundays, or sermon series about the sacrament
- as retreat themes for worship teams or caregiving/visiting teams
- as church newsletter articles

The Hymns

- for congregational singing
- as a solo or a choral anthem
- as responsive prayers
- Text permissions: The original hymn texts in this resource may be reprinted, for not-for-profit use only and without change, for the purpose of use within Christian ministry; author credit must be included with the reprinted hymn texts.
- Tune permissions: With two exceptions, existing hymn tunes and meters are provided as suggestions to pair with the original texts. Many hymnals have tune and metrical indexes. We especially commend the online resource, hymnary.org, to search the suggested hymn tunes and find lists of hymnals that publish them. In addition, feel free to find alternate tunes to fit the hymn texts, write original tunes, or arrange old melodies from different musical genres. The two original hymn tunes/accompaniments may be reprinted from this resource, without change and with full credit, for not-for-profit use in the context of Christian ministry.

The Prayers and Liturgies

- in an order of Communion
- as liturgy/prayer for a themed worship service (such as hunger and feeding)
- as writing or discussion prompts
- Permissions: The prayers and liturgies in this resource may be reprinted, for not-for-profit use only and without change, in the context of Christian ministry; author credit must be included with the reprinted texts.

WHAT IF NO ONE REMEMBERS?

Communion and Memory

Refusing to Forget

MARY LUTI

[Jesus] took bread, and after giving thanks, he broke it and gave it to them, saying, "This is my body, given for you. Do this in remembrance of me." And he did the same with the cup after supper. (Luke 22:19-20, adapted)

When Christians talk about Communion, we say it's a remembrance of Jesus, a memorial. Which is true, but also potentially misleading, as if what we're doing at the table is reminiscing, like you would at a wake.

But in the Gospel's original Greek, the word for remembrance is stronger, edgier, more demanding—*anamnesis*—literally, "against amnesia." It turns out that remembering Jesus in Communion is oppositional, like standing up to something, like standing against an adversary. Remembering at the table is not reminiscence; it's resistance. It's refusing to forget.

There are forces around us and within us that want us to forget what they've been up to for eons, wreaking havoc, taking up all the breathing room, squeezing the life out of everything for ego, profit, supremacy, and power. Killing for sport.

They're still at it, night and day, trying to fog over all traces of Jesus' love revolution in the world and in our hearts. They hope we'll lose his trail, his story's thread. They hope we'll forget we ever knew him.

For if we forget, we'll be putty in their hands. If we forget, they can tell us anything they want, and we won't know they're lying. In the vacuum of forgetting, injustice has it easy, violence rules the day.

Communion is dangerous memory: it's our uprising. At the table we take a stand. We remember him. We remember each other. We remember everyone and everything hate wants to erase. We refuse to forget.

We Will Not Forget You, Jesus

WORDS: **MARY LUTI**
MUSIC: **JODI HITZHUSEN**

We will not forget you, Jesus,
we will not forget.
We will tell your danger story
at this table met:
how you lived in truth unbending,
faithful through the awful ending,
love the reason, love the debt,
we will not forget.

We will not forget you, Jesus,
we will not forget
all the shamed and all the slaughtered,
all who cried for breath.
Every victim has a place here,
they will never be erased here;
singing resurrection's threat,
we will not forget.

We will not forget you, Jesus,
we will not forget.
When the world conspires to make us
lose your story's thread,
we will come and eat, defiant,
revolution's bread of triumph,
hearts shored up and faces set,
we will not forget.

We will not forget you, Jesus,
we will not forget.
When we eat this meal together,
bless and break the bread,
you are here with us in power,

now the day and now the hour,
rising, rising from the dead,
we will not forget.

—

Suggested use before Communion or as part of the Communion prayer with different verses punctuating spoken prayers. It might be effective also as a statement of faith on a Communion Sunday or as part of a special congregational act of commitment to justice-seeking.

We Will Not Forget You, Jesus

*repeat verse 1 until To Coda

Telling the Danger Story

MARY LUTI

PRAISE AND THANKS

We praise you, God, for this table set in love for all who seek you.
Praise, too, for this company, heaven and earth assembled for the feast.
Praise for the mercy we find here, your mothering arms embracing all.

Aware of our failings and grateful for your kindness,
we ask help for our hearts, that we may grow in love
and serve with our whole lives
the purposes of your mercy and the cause of justice.

Mindful also of everyone whose lives are marred
    by exclusion and pain,
we thank you for the joy we find in your house.
We call to mind every victim shamed and slaughtered
    by the world's powers,
every person who cries for breath.
With them, present at this table, we will tell again
the dangerous story of love triumphant over death.

REMEMBERING JESUS

Now, O God, with grateful joy, we remember Jesus.
He sided with the poor, made the sick well,
welcomed sinners, and ate with outcasts.

We remember, we refuse to forget.

He would not hate. He told the truth at the cost of his life.

We remember, we refuse to forget.

Betrayed and deserted by his friends,
he was killed as a common criminal, shamed and despised.

We remember, we refuse to forget.

Death could not hold him. God raised him in power from the grave.

We remember, we refuse to forget.

He returned to us without vengeance, only mercy in his hands.
He is with us now, to the end of the age.

We remember, we refuse to forget.

And we remember that on the night of betrayal,
he fed us with signs of love: a loaf, divided and shared;
a cup, poured and passed from hand to hand;
a meal to eat in resistance,
grace and courage for the struggle that goes on.

"Whenever you do this," he said, "remember me."

PRAYER TO THE HOLY SPIRIT

Come, Holy Spirit, Life of our life!
Bless this grain from the earth, this fruit of the vine.
Make them food and drink of abundant life.

As we share this meal,
help us rejoice that Christ is present with us here.
Give us love for one another,
and make us servants of peace
until your new age of justice comes
and every creature beholds it.

SHARING THE BREAD AND CUP

People are welcomed to the table and Communion is distributed.

Let us give thanks for all we have received.

Thank you, gracious God, for life in the Spirit of Jesus:
for the witness we cannot forget
and the mission of justice you have made our own.
Give us the gifts of Holy Communion:
oneness of heart, love for neighbors, forgiveness of enemies,
the will to serve you every day, and life that never ends.
In Jesus' name we pray. Amen.

Tell the Truth

MARY LUTI

Remember Jesus Christ, raised from the dead, descended from David. This is my gospel… (2 Timothy 2:8, NIV)

I once saw an engraving of saints in heaven hovering over an earthly Communion table. It made an impression. Now when I'm at the table I sense it's not just us in the room. We're remembering Jesus with a community that stretches around the world, and beyond space and time.

It's more than a nice spiritual thought. Consider this, from Margaret Bendroth, *The Spiritual Practice of Remembering:*

"Shortly before he invaded Poland in 1939, Hitler reminded his staff of the Armenian genocide, 24 years earlier—a horror largely invisible to the outside world because those who knew about it chose to say and do nothing. He assured his generals that no one remembered it. And no one had ever paid a moral price for it. There'd be none to pay for this invasion either, he said, not in a world with such a short, self-serving memory."

Bendroth concludes, "The world's unwillingness to remember one genocide will always enable the next." In other words, remembering is an ethical act, a justice imperative. Whenever we gather for Communion, we're duty bound to remember in such a way that what was done to Jesus is never done again. To anyone.

Now, we tend to remember in ways that make us look good, absolve us, support our side. But for truthful remembering, we need more than our own memories alone. We need a community to remember with. And not just a local, like-minded community, but the vast communion of saints.

For if what we remember is partial or local, we'll let ourselves believe, as Bendroth notes, that the bigoted, violent past has nothing to do with us. We might believe that we're not the kind of people who would burn witches or look away from holocausts or criminalize the poor or enslave other human beings. Or turn Jesus in. Or lynch him on a cross.

But with the communion of saints won't let us lie. They'll say, "Well, sadly, a lot of us were that kind of people. You're not immune from all that any more than we were."

If we're ever in need of a bracing corrective to our moral amnesia, our false sense of superiority and innocence—and we always are—we'll find it at the table, remembering in communion with our whole sinful saintly family. Eating the meal together, we'll lend each other wisdom and strength to lift the lamp of truthful, humbling, ethical witness in the world.

Remember Me, You Said

WORDS: **MARY LUTI**
TUNES: **HEARTBEAT (JANE MARSHALL), ROBERT (MARGARET TUCKER)**
10.11.10.11.

Remember me, you said, and so we come
to eat the bread and tell again your story;
remembering whole, your anguish and your joy,
your shaming death and resurrection glory.

Remember me, you said, and so we come
to drink the cup, and meet you in the sharing;
remembering whole, our faithfulness and fear,
our love and hate, our harming and repairing.

And if we shy from memories that accuse,
your saints assembled help us, kind and knowing,
and lend our hearts the courage to be true
and keep the light of witness bravely glowing.

Remember me, you said, and so we come
to eat with thanks this memory meal together,
upheld in hope and bound in love's embrace
with saints of every age, now and forever.

Suggested use as part of the confession and assurance before Communion. It is especially appropriate on All Saints Day.

Not Just Us

MARY LUTI

PRAISE AND THANKS

Generous Love,
you set the table long and wide and beautiful,
with places not just for us alone, but for everyone,
saints and sinners of all times and places.

For you know how much we need each other,
how much the consolation of company means to us,
how good it is to join the present and the past,
how much deeper the love, sharper the vision,
more complete the memory,
and more authentic the witness
when it's not just us alone.

In awe of your mercy, we ask you to unite us in peace,
as we remember Jesus, your greatest gift to us.

REMEMBERING JESUS

We remember the way he witnessed to your justice,
shared your mercy, told the truth, and risked everything for it.
We remember his terrible death and his indestructible new life.

We remember that he called us to follow him.

We remember all his precious siblings, living and dead,
whom he has made our siblings, too,
and all whose lives cry out for justice and hope.
They are present here: we embrace them, never forgetting.

We remember the glory and the pain,
the harm and the healing,

**what we have done and left undone,
in thoughts, words, and deeds,
our costly faithfulness and our timid failings.**

Asking for your mercy, and confident of your love,
we come now to eat the meal
that strengthens our bonds of affection
and our ties of accountability:
the meal of bread and body,
the meal of cup and poured out life;
the meal of persevering presence,
of Love that rejoices in our good
and redeems our failings.

PRAYER TO THE HOLY SPIRIT

**Holy Spirit, bless what we do here in Jesus' name,
sharing with each other his bread and cup.
Help us meet him in this Communion,
rejoicing in his affectionate company:
not just us alone, but all of us together,
here and everywhere, now and forever. Amen.**

When Jesus Calls His Friends to Eat

WORDS: **MARY LUTI**
TUNE: **DANIEL (IRISH), PRAISE GOD (HOPSON)**
8.8.8.8.

When Jesus calls his friends to eat,
God's Spirit searches far and wide;
she finds us all and brings us home
for sweet communion side by side.

In numbers small, in powers slight,
in short supply the church appears;
but faith perceives what eyes can't see:
the universe is gathered here.

Here, all the living and the dead,
here, all the saints and angels blessed;
and in profusion, honored guests:
the meek, the shunned, the poor oppressed.

God's church assembles for the Feast
in numbers countless and unknown,
so in this house where Love presides
no child need ever eat alone.

Unbounded by our human time,
untethered to one little space,
God dreams a dream, and it comes true:
for all, belonging and a place!

Suggested use as part of a celebration of the "cloud of witnesses" gathered at the table, such as All Saints Day. Try alternating verses with young voices and older voices, high voices and low voices, choir and congregation, etc.

We Are One

KENNETH L. SAMUEL

Holy God, in this Communion, we are one:

One in the witness of those present with us and those present around us, who testify to your healing presence, your saving grace, your resurrecting power.

One in the work you have given us to be agents of reconciliation in this world of partisanship and polarization.

One in your worship, true and living God, whose good news of all-inclusive love we celebrate and announce to all in word and in deed.

Holy God, in this Communion, we are one:

One in the community of disciples, who overcome fear through faith, and who allow the truth about ourselves to make us free.

One in the community of freedom fighters, whose conviction and courage bring down the strongholds of injustice and iniquity.

One in the community of believers, whose loving relations in the household of faith make this Communion holy.

Holy God, in this Communion, we are one:

One, in the purposeful providence of our Creator.
One, in the trusted salvation of our Redeemer.
One, in the glorious promise of our Sustainer.
In you, O God, we are one.

IT'S NOT THE SAME WITHOUT YOU

Communion and Belonging

Wait for Each Other

MARY LUTI

When you come together in one place, it is not to eat the Lord's supper, for each of you goes ahead with your own supper. Thus some go hungry while others get drunk. Why do you make those who have nothing feel ashamed? My siblings, no: when you come together to eat, wait for each other. (1 Corinthians 11:21-22, 33, adapted)

Waiting to eat until everyone is seated is simply polite. But Paul isn't talking about etiquette here. He's warning us not to desecrate the Lord's Supper, pointing out the difference between that Supper and our own meals, between Christ's table and the world's.

At the world's table, no one waits for anyone. It's a demented scramble to be first, shoving others aside, stepping over bodies. Be first and you get prime cuts and excellent wine. Limp in later, you get gristle and dregs. At the world's table, the wealthy, the privileged, and the strong devour everyone else's share of the feast of life. But at Jesus' table, mutual deference is the sacrament's outward sign every bit as much as bread and wine.

We eat the Lord's Supper most faithfully not when we're morally pure or doctrinally sound, but when we're giving no advantage to the privileged. When in deeds personal and political we refuse to shame the poor. When our own wellbeing is inseparable from others'. When we set welcome tables in the streets of our grasping, unequal world as intentionally and as we set Communion tables in our sanctuaries.

It's the Lord's Supper most faithfully when we wait for each other. When we wait and work and witness until everyone arrives, everyone is welcomed, everyone is seated, served, and fed.

Who's Seated at the Table?

WORDS: **MARY LUTI**
TUNES: **WEST MAIN, WEDLOCK, SALLEY GARDEN**
7.6.7.6.D

Who's seated at the table,
who has a waiting place?
Who's always warmly welcome
in Love's most kind embrace?
Who finds a dear belonging,
who's home, who's home at last?
Who's treasured here and honored,
no questions ever asked?

And who is Jesus missing?
Whose absence deeply pains?
For whom is Love still pining,
what searching work remains?
What work of peace and pardon,
what justice to increase?
What beauty to discover,
what singing joy release?

The feast of great thanksgiving,
the song, the memory.
The bread, the wine, the story,
Christ's precious company.
The table set in mercy,
no bar, no lock, no gate.
Who's seated at the table?
All earth and heaven wait.

Suggested use for any Communion service, but especially when a congregation is exploring the scope and character of its Christian welcome. See also its use in the exercise, "Who's Seated at the Table?"

Who's Seated at the Table? Collaboratively Creating Communion

KAJI DOUŠA

This activity cultivates shared meaning by means of collaborative input. It can be engaged in person during worship, or as a thoughtful survey that encourages people to reflect and share. Invite all your people to participate. Cast a wide net. Expect richness across generations.

1. Invite reflection on the questions in the first verse of the hymn, "Who's Seated at the Table":

   Who's seated at the table, who has a waiting place? Who's always warmly welcome in Love's most kind embrace? Who finds a dear belonging, who's home, who's home at last? Who's treasured here and honored, no questions ever asked?

   Then ask: In our community, who do you see at the table?

2. Next, invite reflection on verse 2.

   And who is Jesus missing? Whose absence deeply pains? For whom is Love still pining, what searching work remains? What work of peace and pardon, what justice to increase? What beauty to discover, what singing joy release?

   Then ask: In our community, who do you not see at the table?

3. Finally, invite reflection on the final question in verse 3.

   Who's seated at the table? All earth and heaven wait.

   Then ask: If it's true that heaven and earth are waiting for a world without gates and a table without bars, what prayer would you offer to open this community's welcome even wider?

4. If people are writing their responses, gather and read them; and/or listen as oral responses are shared. Try to receive the spirit and language of each offering as a gift. Notice what draws you in and what you'd prefer to discard or think more about. Treat the offered words as holy. Find the words you want to share in worship. You may have enough for several liturgies here! You can incorporate the responses into the following liturgy.

INVITATION

Beloved in Christ, you are welcome here. You are welcome, *[incorporate responses to #1].*
We give thanks that Jesus sets a table so wide and gives a welcome so complete
that we now come to drink the cup of joy and eat with thanks the bread of life he gives.

CONFESSION

We know, O God, that our own habits and fears set limits that you do not place.
We acknowledge this, remembering: *[incorporate responses to #2]*
and all who pine for our love but do not experience it.
As we call all this to mind, we cast this failing onto your love and mercy.

ASSURANCE

God gives you peace and pardon,
forgiveness and healing, now and forever.
Your sins are forgiven.

PRAYER OF THANKSGIVING AND WORDS OF INSTITUTION

[Here offer thanks for God's goodness to us, and tell the story of Jesus, his companions, and the gift of bread and wine.]

PRAYER TO THE HOLY SPIRIT

Let us pray:
Send us your Holy Spirit, O God,
and bless these gifts of bread and cup.
May they be for us the very life of Christ.
May they help us to: *[incorporate prayers from #3].*
We ask this in the name of Jesus, who taught us to pray:

THE LORD'S PRAYER

INVITATION

Hallelujah! We eat Christ's Supper true. The feast is before us. *[Communion is distributed.]*

THANKSGIVING

We give you thanks, O God,
for this feast of great thanksgiving.
We thank you for the song. We thank you for the memory.
We thank you for the bread, the wine, the story.
We thank you for Christ's precious company.
Thank you for this table set in mercy,
for which there is no bar, no lock, no gate.
With all earth and heaven, we wait.
In Jesus' name. Amen.

Guests Among Guests

MARY LUTI

Jesus went out and saw a tax collector by the name of Levi sitting at his tax booth. "Follow me," Jesus said to him, and Levi got up… Then Levi held a great banquet for Jesus at his house… (Luke 5:27-29, NIV)

I find only three instances in scripture when Jesus hosts a meal—the improvised feeding of the multitudes, the members-only Last Supper, and the post-resurrection breakfast for a handful of frustrated disciple-fishermen.

Other than that, Jesus doesn't host anyone at his table. He doesn't have a table. He's always at someone else's. Tax collectors like Levi and Zacchaeus throw him banquets. Pharisees, too. Peter's wife feeds him at her house. And Martha, in Bethany. Jesus doesn't invite; he gets invited.

So when we say we welcome everyone to the church's table because Jesus welcomed everyone to his, we're on shaky evidentiary ground. Which doesn't argue for exclusion. It only suggests that Jesus may present a challenge to us—not so much because he was a gracious host, but because he was a willing guest.

If our churches aren't very inclusive, it might be because too many of us have mistaken ourselves for the Giver of the Feast. We're not hosts extending invitations. We're guests among guests. Yet we behave as if arriving earlier than others has given us proprietary rights over the hall. Which means we haven't yet pondered deeply enough the Mercy by which we all got in here in the first place.

Our churches will more closely resemble God's all-embracing realm when we relinquish our sense of entitlement to them, cease welcoming others as if there's no such a thing as "others," stop playing munificent hosts, and learn to be good guests.

Who Hosts and Who Guests?

DONNA SCHAPER

We know, O God,
that we are both hosts and guests at this table.
We know, too, that guests are often hosts,
and hosts are often guests,
and that you like to mix these roles up
in a great welcoming act of eating together
to remember you.
Come, Holy Spirit, come.
Join us at our table
as we join you at yours. Amen.

Christ of Food and Every Pleasure

WORDS: **MARY LUTI**
TUNES: **JULION, FORTUNATUS (NEW)**
8.7.8.7.8.7.

Christ of food and every pleasure,
you have longed to eat this feast!
Now we're gathered here together,
high and mighty, low and least,
to receive your joy unmeasured
and to make your joy complete.

No one owns this great partaking,
no one's higher than the rest;
every privilege here forsaking,
even you, O Christ, a guest:
all are one in Love's inbreaking
at this table manifest.

In this circle of God's dreaming
boundless welcome comes to earth.
Free of coveting and scheming,
free of worried rank and worth,
guests alike here, glad and gleaming,
eat and drink to our rebirth.

Suggested use as a hymn for general use on Communion Sundays to recall the inherent equality of every person at the table.

Everyone a Guest

MARY LUTI

INVITATION

Jesus accepted invitations from everyone
and ate at many tables.
He was not often the host,
he was a guest among guests.
At this table where we remember him,
we too are not hosts.
We are all guests,
all invited by Mercy, all summoned by Love.
Come, then, everyone, and enjoy Love's hospitality.
Lay aside any need you have to be first or best,
or to decide who is worthy to come and eat.
Just be grateful to be here,
and open your hearts to praise:

THANKS AND PRAISE

God most generous and kind,
the reach of your mercy is endless.
You find us all, wherever we are,
and bring us to your table.
Your guest list is as unrestricted as your love.
For the gracious welcome we have all received,
whether we came first or last, early or late,
with hands full of gifts, or with nothing at all,
we praise you, singing your glory, this day and forever:

SANCTUS

Holy, holy, holy... *[or another brief song of praise]*.

REMEMBERING JESUS

Now, O God, we remember Jesus.
We remember that he ate with Simon the Pharisee,
with Zacchaeus the tax collector,
and in Peter's house after making his mother well.

We remember that he ate in Bethany with Mary and Martha,
and their brother, Lazarus, whom he summoned from the grave.
We remember that he ate with rich and poor,
righteous people and sinners,
friends, deniers, doubters, and betrayers.

He told us not to take the best seats at banquets,
but to defer to others; to be good guests.

THE STORY OF THE BREAD AND CUP

And we remember that on the night of his betrayal,
he ate again with his disciples in an upper room.

He shared blessed bread with them
and poured out wine, signs of his coming death,
signs of a life determined to love despite the risk.

Whenever we eat, with whomever we eat,
as guests among guests, we remember him.
He is with us always, to the end of the age.

PRAYER TO THE HOLY SPIRIT

Come, Holy Spirit, come!
Bless this bread and this fruit of the vine.
By our eating and drinking, open our hearts
to other guests you are always inviting,
so that one day everyone who hungers
will have an honored place in your house,
the best seats at your table.

[The people are invited, and Communion is distributed.]

THANKSGIVING

Thank you, God,
for inviting us to this Banquet of Life.
and feeding us with the good news of Jesus
and his wondrous bread and cup.
You are always glad to have us here
around your family table.

Help us notice who is missing.
Make us everybody's neighbor.
Send us to them as friends
with your standing invitation to come,
to eat, to know love, and be in peace at home.

Not a Test

MARY LUTI

You open your hand and satisfy the desire of every living thing. (Psalm 145:16, NIV)

Over the years I've heard a lot of painful stories of rejection by the church. Most were about being denied Communion. Divorced people. Trans people. People who attended church but weren't baptized. Members of the wrong denomination. People with intellectual disabilities.

One person's pastor told him that his presence in the Communion line was upsetting to people—he was badly disfigured from a fire—so would he mind coming after church, alone? He left and never came back.

Years ago, a woman with an eating disorder told me she starved herself because she didn't deserve to eat. She would eat again only when she got thinner and prettier and felt worthy enough. That day hasn't come yet.

She stopped going to Communion, too. She'd been taught that Communion was holy food, food for the good and worthy. She wasn't good or worthy.

Listening to her, it struck me that when a church—any church—tells someone who wants Communion, "No, not you," its voice isn't all that different from the inner voice of an eating disorder that tells sufferers they can eat only when they've passed the test.

I once read an essay in which the author, in recovery herself, described eating as "a terror-laden battlefield of shame, secrecy, and guilt," a constant reminder of being unworthy and unloved. But unlike the woman who spoke to me years ago, she had returned to Communion. She knew it might not do so for everyone, but it was helping her heal.

Communion offered her a different definition of what food is—a gift, not a test. She'd first grasped this sheer graciousness when worshiping at a church with an open table. Nothing was said there about worth, only an open-handed invitation from an all-satisfying God.

So many people experience food as a stand-in for worth. Or a reward for virtue. Or a confirmation of good standing. Communion isn't that kind of food. If it ever becomes that kind of food in your church, you'll all need to repent and start over. Because, as that writer concluded, "The Church can't be a source of healing if it behaves like an illness."

I Know You Can't Believe

WORDS: **MARY LUTI**
TUNE: **BOROUGH (CYRIL V. TAYLOR)**
10.10.10.10

I know you can't believe I love you so.
I know you fear you never will be fine.
I know you think you don't deserve a thing,
but I'm telling you, beloved, you are mine.

I want to give you all my hope and joy.
I want to bless your life in every part.
I want to show you how you shine and shine,
and I'm telling you, beloved, you're my heart.

I know they said this Meal is not for you.
I know too often it has been a test.
I know you think that you might never pass,
but I'm telling you, beloved, you can rest.

You are the one this bread is waiting for.
You are the one for whom the wine pours free.
You are the one whose place I've saved and set,
and I welcome you, beloved: taste and see.

Suggested use as an invitation at the start of a Communion liturgy, or immediately before the sacrament is distributed and received. This hymn is written in Christ's voice as encouragement for people who have been expressly excluded for not measuring up, or who have excluded themselves from the table with doubts about worthiness, but it encompasses us all, who at one time or another have felt we did not deserve the gift.

It's Not the Same without You

LIZ MILLER

INVITATION

There are too many places in our world
where the price of admission is more than we can afford,
where we are asked to leave pieces of ourselves at the door,
where we are told there's no room for one more.

At this Communion table there's always room, room to spare.
Yes, we will squeeze you in right over there.
Take a seat, pull up a stool or your wheelchair,
settle in a pew or on a cushion square.

This is a table that is not just a table.
It is the sign of God's love here on earth,
an affirmation of your sacred worth.

This is a table that, whether we are many or few,
would not be the same if it didn't include you.

THANKS AND PRAISE

We give thanks to you, O God,
for drawing us close,
for feeding our bodies,
for nurturing our spirits,
for loving us exactly as we are.

We carry within us memories
of rejection and loneliness,
shame and self-loathing, guilt and fear.
And so we give thanks that at your table
we embody a different message:

We are beloved.
We are enough.
We are worthy.

We feast together with gratitude,
hungry to build a world
where every body is honored,
where every bruised and broken spirit is healed,
where everyone is invited to receive
the gift of unconditional love.

REMEMBERING JESUS

We remember that night in the upper room,
Jesus at a table crowded with disciples.
He knew their pasts, the places that had formed them.
He knew their future, the pain and sorrow to come.
He saw the places deep within
that they tried to keep hidden,
and still he offered them
the cup of salvation and the bread of life,
gifts to show them they are loved, always loved.

PRAYER TO THE HOLY SPIRIT

Come, Holy Spirit, come,
transform these ordinary things
into sacred gifts.

Prepare our bodies to be fed.
Prepare our hearts to receive a love
that is more persistent than fear,
and a life stronger than death.

INVITATION TO THE TABLE

The table is ready.
Come to feast,

come to be known,
come to receive God's grace.

THANKSGIVING

Let's say thanks for all we have received.

Thanks be to God whose name is Love.
Thanks be to God who hungers
to know us and be known by us.
As we leave this table,
may we carry with us a taste
of the inherent worth and dignity of every person,
offering the same to all we meet. Amen.

BEARING FRUIT

Communion, Creation and Labor

Vine and Branches

MARY LUTI

"I am the vine; you are the branches. If you remain in me, and I in you, you will bear much fruit." (John 15:5, NIV)

Jesus calls himself the vine and his disciples the branches that bear fruit. The Church has always heard a reference to the Eucharist in this saying, especially to the cup we bless. From ancient times, the wine in the cup has stood for the lifeblood of Jesus circulating through the church like nourishing sap, uniting Teacher and disciples in one common life, generative and strong, a holy communion.

But the metaphor of vine and branches is not just about communing with Jesus and each other. It's also about communing with the natural world. To belong to the One who adopted our flesh, and to belong to all our human neighbors, is also to belong to Earth. The more entwined we are in each other, the healthier and more fruitful we become.

It's not for nothing that every Christian ritual of inclusion and acceptance, pardon and peace, healing and nourishment requires us to touch earthy things and to let them touch us. In Baptism, it's water and, in some parts of the Church, salt, oil, and beeswax. For healing, we use anointing oil and reverent human touch. In Communion, it's wheat and grape. Through them all, the grace of loving Presence materializes. By earthy things we learn how precious and loved we are, in body as well as soul.

We are not the only stewards within God's creation. The earth itself is a steward, caring for us as much as we care for the earth. It's an irreplaceable gift to our whole selves, mediating divine healing and peace to every part. Without these gifts, we would never know the sight, taste, sound, aroma, and touch of the invisible God.

We owe Earth care not just because it's in our self-interest (although it is), but also because it's the beloved medium of God's self-showing, revealing the Holy One to our senses in beauty, in nourishment, in joy.

When We Eat Bread, We Eat the Soil and Sun

WORDS: **MARY LUTI**
TUNES: **CLIFF TOWN, SHELDONIAN**
10.10.10.10

"If Christ is the body of God, then the bread he offers is also the body of the cosmos. Look deeply and you notice the sunshine in the bread, the blue sky in the bread, the cloud and the great earth in the bread. You eat it in such a way that you become alive, truly alive." (Thich Nhat Hanh)

When we eat bread, we eat the soil and sun,
the quiet winter rest, the surge of spring;
we eat the summer heat, the clouds and rain,
and every breeze that makes the meadows sing.

When we drink wine, we drink the soil and sun,
we drink the tendril's curl, the pruning grief;
the green, the deepest purple, and the pale,
the swelling cluster and the shady leaf.

When we receive Communion's wine and bread,
the Earth enfolds us as her very own;
we eat and drink the Life that gives us life;
to every sense Love makes its presence known.

Now as we eat the sun and drink the rain,
and praise you, God, for Earth and all her care,
let thanks and reverence ripen in the hands
we lend to her protection and repair.

Suggested use for Communion on Creation Sunday, Earth Day, or any Communion service when themes of creation and environmental justice are being explored.

In Praise of Earth

MOLLY PHINNEY BASKETTE

INVITATION

To paraphrase Mary Oliver,
you do not have to be good to receive the gift of this meal.
You do not have to walk on your knees
for a hundred miles through the desert repenting.
You only have to let the soft animal of your body love what it loves.

We are animals who need care and feeding.
To acknowledge our animal natures and needs
is to acknowledge the dignity and worth of every created thing.

To take this meal is to take our proper place in the rhythms of our Earth,
to acknowledge our right-sized place in the ecosystem.

To eat this food is to acknowledge our belonging
in the great unrolling dance of Creation
from the dawn of the universe until its ending.

Come, then, everyone, and be where you belong.

PRAISE AND THANKS

God, through the wonder of photosynthesis,
you turn sunlight and soil
into fruit of the vine and grain of the field.

Add yeast for rising, salt for flavor, water for life,
then knead, bake, and ferment
until these elements become food for body and spirit.

God, you are in all things, and therefore in us.
God, we are in all things, atoms sprung from stardust,

repurposed for a moment in a too-short human lifespan,
then repurposed again.
We acknowledge the holiness of this bread and cup,
the holiness of you and us and everything in this meal.

BREAD AND CUP

Now, God, we remember:
On the last night of his life,
Jesus went back to the most basic need
all living things share—to eat.

He took a loaf, Brother Bread,
and when he had thanked you for it,
he shared it among all those gathered, saying,
Take this and eat. This is my Body, given for you.
Good bread for healing and joy.

Likewise after supper, he took a cup, Sister Wine,
a symbol of life, and joy, and the wheel of fate.
When he had thanked you for it, he said to his disciples,
Take this and drink: this cup seals a new covenant.
Lifeblood for healing and joy.

In eating and drinking, we acknowledge with thanks
our covenant with all created things
to heal and tend and foster growth,
and not to deplete or destroy.

THANKSGIVING

Thank you, thank you, thank you, God,
for making grape and wheat
and sun and rain
and us ourselves.
Thank you for the gift of life!
May we tend that life, your life,
in all living things and the Earth itself. Amen.

Entwined

DONNA SCHAPER

Twine and Vine us, Almighty God, in such a way
that we forget which part we are.
Bring us close to you in this Holy Communion.
Let us feel your presence.
May you know our presence, too.
Help us to practice this presence of the Holy,
not just while eating and drinking
the things of earth at a sacred meal,
but every time we dare to eat. Amen.

No Work, No Communion

MARY LUTI

Behold, the wages you withheld from the workers who harvested your fields are crying aloud, and the cries of the harvesters have reached the ears of the Lord of hosts. (James 5:4, NAB)

Basil Hume, the former archbishop of Westminster, once noted, "No work, no Communion." In other words, there's no bread and wine to bless unless someone labors to make it. Communion begins long before the service in church begins, in the daily work of human beings as workers plant, harvest, mill, bake, pluck, press, ferment, refine, and bottle.

Communion is a divine gift, but human work is the medium through which it arrives on our tables to be shared in love. Like all human labor, the work that makes Communion is holy work, and whenever we gather for Communion we should gratefully acknowledge its dignity. We should examine our consciences, too. For to receive the gift of someone else's labor is a confession as much as a celebration.

By regularly consuming the labor that makes Communion, we're meant to become the kind of people who don't just spout pieties about the dignity of labor, but who can also face the fact that holy human work is often unsafe and rarely justly compensated. The kind of people who know that the bread and juice on our table, like so many products we routinely consume, are often the products of human suffering—and that we're all implicated in this injustice.

And more. The human suffering the Communion elements signify is intimately tied up with Earth's impoverishment and suffering, too—pollution, deforestation, ecological imbalances, unchecked free markets that destroy the health of people and planet for the sake of profit. All this is in the bread and cup: the sweating, suffering, suffocating bodies and blood of human beings, and the damaged exhaustion of the beautiful, plentiful world we were given to tend.

At Communion we routinely pray that the bread and cup will become for us the food and drink of abundant life. Let's pray, too, that by eating and drinking, we'll also be transformed—communionized—into a people dedicated to ensuring an equal and generous sharing of the world's goods for all; respect for those who labor; and care for Earth, our common home.

The Wheat in Our Bread

WORDS: **MARY LUTI**
TUNE: **SAMANTHRA**
11.8.11.8.D

The wheat in our bread is a gift of the earth
the product of soil, sun, and rain;
but labor was needed to make it a loaf,
to bring it to table from grain.
And some workers planted and some workers tilled,
some harvested long in the heat,
some took it by tons to the market to sell,
some kneaded and baked it to eat.

The grape in our cup is a gift of the earth,
the product of soil, rain, and shine;
but labor was needed to make it a drink,
to bring it to table from vine.
And some workers pruned and some gathered the fruit,
some pressed it, some racked and refined;
some barreled and aged it and left it a while,
to ripen its joy in due time.

Alive at this table, our host and our feast,
good Jesus is ready to bless
the fruits of the earth we are privileged to share,
the products of thresher and press.
And while we're all eating with thanks in our hearts,
we promise we'll never forget
the justice we owe to all people who work,
and work to repay them our debt.

Suggested use for Communion on Labor Day weekend (U.S.) or any Communion service in which themes of the dignity of work, workers' rights, or the connections between labor, consumption, and the environment are being explored.

God at Work

MATT LANEY

WELCOME

The Spirit is laboring today.
Grace is rolling up her sleeves.
We give thanks for the work of Christ
who toils on our behalf.
It is right and just to lift up
all who water the earth with their sweat.
And so we pray:

THANKS AND PRAISE

Wonder worker, we gather on stolen land, at a table we did not make, to receive bread we did not bake, to satisfy an ache we alone cannot shake.

We come, tired from our own labors, overwrought and worn thin, to remember and receive the life-giving work of Jesus.

On the night he was betrayed, Jesus got up from the table.
He bent before his friends like a servant, and washed their feet, saying,
"Unless you let me do this for you, you can have no part of me."

He also took bread, blessed it, divided it, and handed it to them, saying,
"Take, eat, this is my body, broken for you."

He also filled his cup, gave thanks for it, and gave it to them, saying,
"Take, drink, this is my lifeblood, poured out for you."

"As often as you eat this bread and drink this cup
you celebrate my lifework until it is complete."

PRAYER TO THE HOLY SPIRIT

Spirit of labor and of rest,
may your presence rest here, on this table, on these gifts.
As we receive them, may we also receive and celebrate
all the labor you have expended on our behalf,
your creating love given freely and without conditions.

INVITATION

Ministering to you in the name of Jesus,
you are welcome to taste and see the goodness of God.

THANKSGIVING AFTER RECEIVING

Holy Provider, Grace made tangible, Love in motion,
we have received your gifts with thanks in our hearts.
Grateful for the labor that produced them,
we promise we'll never forget
the justice we owe to all people who work, and work
to repay them our debt.

Gifts and Labor

MARY LUTI

We spread your table with these gifts of the earth and of our labor. (UCC Book of Worship, Service of Word and Sacrament I)

A friend of mine is a deacon in a church with a bread-making ministry that provides fresh loaves for weekly Communion. They always freeze some, too, for long holiday weekends when the team doesn't bake.

One such weekend, he arrived early to pop a frozen loaf into the microwave. But there were no loaves to pop. Somebody forgot to stock the freezer. There was a grocery store nearby, so he dashed out, snatched a loaf off the shelf, and was back in no time.

Removing the wrapper, it hit him. How lovely the bread-making ministry was. How devoted the team's labor. Their joy. Once he'd heard them singing as they worked. And their bread was delicious. He wondered about the people who'd made the store-bought bread, all the workers who'd planted, reaped, milled, baked, packaged, distributed, and stocked it. Did they feel satisfied, too?

The mass-produced bread bothered him. And it moved him. During the service he was distracted, thinking about production and land use, fair wages and working conditions, marketing and prices, distribution and access. He hoped it wasn't sacrilegious to be thinking about economics right before receiving Christ's Body. He also wondered if it was sacrilegious not to think about such things.

When the pastor lifted the loaf and said the usual words from the book, "...gift of the earth and of our labor," it stung him. He'd heard them before, but not so clearly what they imply. Not so clearly what they demand. He wondered what took him so long.

For Earth Day, Creation Sunday

MARY LUTI

"To live, we must daily break the body and shed the blood of Creation. When we do this knowingly, lovingly, skillfully, reverently, it is a sacrament. When we do it ignorantly, greedily, clumsily, destructively, it is a desecration. In such desecration we condemn ourselves to spiritual and moral loneliness, and others to want." (Wendell Berry)

INVITATION

In the beginning, God made a garden,
and every creature lived in it happily with God.
We took long walks with God in the cool of the evening,
humans and snails, kangaroos and spiders, kitties and larks.

And when we all sat down with God to eat,
the curling vines gave up their fruit,
the tall gold stalk gave up its grain,
and we ate delicious bread and drank from a cup of blessing,
singing songs under stars 'till morning.

And the grateful creation was at peace.

Ever since, whenever we honor the earth
by eating and drinking with heartfelt thanks,
God walks with us again. God sits with us and eats.
Our tables become the garden,
the whole creation sighs with peace,
and we see again how life was meant to be.

Come, now, everyone, to the garden God planted in the East, in Eden.
Come, taste and remember, taste and see how good God is.

Let us pray.

Thank you, Creator God, for sharing your life with us
through every good thing of this world.

Thank you most of all for Jesus,
who sat us down to eat and drink good bread and good wine,
so that in tasting how good they are
we could remember how good you are.

He is our Eden, our Garden of peace.
In him we find the fullness of life you desired for us from the start—
walking together, sharing food, living in peace.

Send the Spirit to this table now where he still sits us down,
where we still remember you.

Bless the bread and the cup,
fruit of the earth and work of our hands.
May they become by your grace
the taste of Eden in our hearts.

As we eat and drink together,
let us behold more clearly the way you intended life to be.

Consecrate us to the work of making it so,
by respecting the earth and sharing its goodness with all,
in reverence and hope, with justice and joy.

SHARING BREAD AND CUP

Dear friends, this is the bread Jesus blessed, broke,
and gave us to share in remembrance of him.
This is the cup Jesus blessed, poured,
and gave us to drink in remembrance of him.
Eating and drinking together,

we remember his life, full of goodness and joy.
We remember his death and refuse its violence.
We remember his rising and rejoice in his resilience.
And we wait with longing for him to come again:
to do justice in mercy,
to welcome in love,
and restore all creation,
to the praise and glory of God.

ONE SKIN, ONE KIN

Communion and Bodies

This Is My Body

MARY LUTI

Then [Jesus] took a loaf of bread, and when he had given thanks, he broke it and gave it to them, saying, "This is my body..." (Luke 22:19, NRSV)

I once gave a talk about Heaven to some church folks. I told them the Bible doesn't say that our souls will float eternally on clouds. It describes instead a transformed creation where we'll live a whole human life together. And a whole human life means, somehow, an embodied life.

Then I said that in that new creation nobody will be sick or disabled. Every body will be made new, healed and whole.

The woman in the wheelchair spoke up. Marian, her name tag said. I hadn't noticed her there. Later she told me it wasn't the first time she'd been invisible. She said, "I've been using this chair for 27 years. It took 20 for me to stop thinking I needed fixing. Don't say I'm not whole. I won't be walking into Heaven, I plan to roll."

Over the years she'd stomached a lot of glib churchy talk about wholeness and healing. The implications were clear: bodies like hers are defective, substandard. But good news—she won't have to lug it around forever. She'll be getting a new, improved version.

It pissed her off. She pointed out that Jesus' resurrection Body still bears the wounds of spear and nails. It's in the gospel. Remember Thomas? "Christ's Body is a disabled body," she said. "Nobody says he's not whole."

It sounded like a speech she'd given a hundred times. Promises of perfection delivered nothing but shame. Unreal talk about physical healing and wholeness dishonored her body. Promises of perfection delivered nothing but shame. She shouldn't have had to shoulder the extra burden of being our teacher that day, too. But she did.

The group asked me to celebrate Holy Communion to close the day. We said prayers, sang songs, passed the peace, read scripture. When I took bread to bless it, she cut in before I could say the words, and said them herself: "This is my Body."

Now We Tell the Ancient Story

WORDS: **MARY LUTI**
TUNE: **RESTORATION (SOUTHERN HARMONY)**
8.7.8.7.

Now we tell the ancient story.
Now we bless the gift of bread.
Now the table shines with glory:
Jesus risen from the dead. *[Repeat the last two lines.]*

Living Jesus, glory glowing,
song of morning, light of stars.
Here in heaven's beauty showing
heaven's hands bear human scars. *[Repeat the last two lines.]*

Life in wonder, life in struggle,
life that death cannot destroy;
in one Body joined and living
scars and glory, wounds and joy. *[Repeat the last two lines.]*

Every body God-befriended,
bearing still its deepest wound;
when all time and death are ended,
shining like the empty tomb. *[Repeat the last two lines.]*

Suggested use as a hymn before Communion to draw attention to embodiment themes, or as a hymn after Communion to celebrate our union with the risen Christ at the table. Individual verses might also be sung as responses to spoken affirmations about the holiness of our bodies: for example, during a prayer of confession, in the people's prayers or pastoral prayer, or as part of another special prayer focusing on the body, human equality, and related justice themes.

One Holy Body

VINCE AMLIN

INVITATION

We eat this meal as one body.
And that one body includes your body.
And it looks like your body.

It has skin like your own. Brown, black.
Scarred, tattooed. Itching, hairy, calloused, sore.

It is fat. Or skinny. Or thick. Or jacked.
It has lost limbs. It was made with extra digits.

It is swirling with desire. Or maybe it isn't.
It loves bodies like your own,
or different from your own, or all bodies, or no bodies.

It aches. It hums. It walks. It cannot move.
It is full of cancer. It is full of another body.
It is becoming another body.

It is Christ's body. Here and now.
The whole church gathered as your body.
Blessed. Broken. Shared.

We eat this meal as one body.
And that one body includes your body.
But it also looks nothing like your body.
But like another body completely different from your own.
Your neighbor's body.
Your enemy's body.

That body, Christ's body. Hosting you. Every body.
Revealing to you the Living God.

Here and now. In this meal.
Every body is welcome.

THANKS AND PRAISE

We begin this way:

God be with you
And also with you.

Lift up your hearts.
We lift them up to God.

Let us give thanks to God.
It is right to give God thanks and praise.

It is right to praise and thank you, God!
You drew our bodies out of the dust,
out of the body of the earth.
And you called them good.
When we were ashamed of our bodies,
you asked us tenderly,
"Who told you that you were naked?"

You heard the cries of our bodies from struggle and captivity.
You broke our chains and set us free.
You took off our shoes and reintroduced us to holy ground.

You sustained our bodies with food and water.
You sustained our bodies with law and worship.

You gave us songs for our throats to sing.
You gave us a call to justice that burns within our bellies.
You gave us work to do for the restoration of a world
that is good for all bodies.

And not satisfied with all that, you became a body.
You breathed. You cried. You ate. You touched. You spat.

You drew. You walked. You fished. You slept.
You loved. You bled. You died. You lived.

And on the night before your death,
you gathered with others for a meal.
Friends, neighbors, enemies.
And during dinner you took a loaf of bread,
and you blessed it. And you broke it.
And you gave it to them, saying,
"This is my body, given for you.
Eat it and remember."

And after dinner you took a cup and gave thanks.
And you passed it around, hand to hand, saying,
"This is my blood, poured out for you.
Drink it and remember."

PRAYER TO THE HOLY SPIRIT

And so we ask, Holy Spirit,
take this food and make it into body.
Take our bodies and make us one body.
Christ's body.
Breathing, crying, spitting, bleeding,
blessing, breaking, sharing,
revealing to all the Living God.
Here and now. Amen.

You Come among Us to Preside

WORDS: **MARY LUTI**
TUNE: **FIDUCIA (ROBINSON), SALVATION (BOYD), KINGSFOLD**
8.6.8.6.D

You come among us to preside
and bless this meal you give.
Here, as we eat, we all become
one body, called to live.
One body, called to live and love
all precious human flesh,
and humbly bow and honor well
its awesome holiness.

For holy was the flesh we bear
and precious in God's sight
when God first fashioned us for joy,
for honor and delight;
and holy still, each body sings
a song of wondrous grace:
that with a body like our own
you lived in time and space.

In time and space, and even more,
when time and space are done,
we'll all be raised in mystery
with you, O Jesus, one.
With you, O Jesus, proud and free
from judgment's lies and shame,
our splendid difference on display,
a map of joy and pain.

One Body marked with joy and pain,
one Body scarred with nails,
one Body made of earth and stars,
all beauty and travail:

we bless and praise and share you now,
as heaven's throng adores,
for you have taken all our flesh
and we have taken yours.

Suggested use as a general Communion hymn, especially during any Communion service focusing on the Incarnation and embodiment themes.

Pie Later

MARY LUTI

The disciples came to Jesus, saying, "Where do you want us to make the preparations for you to eat the Passover?" He said, "Go into the city to a certain man and say to him, 'The Teacher says, My time is near; I will eat the Passover at your house…'" So the disciples did as Jesus directed and prepared the Passover meal. (Matthew 26:17-19, NRSV)

According to *The New York Times*, Americans—who can romanticize just about anything—are fascinated by the last meals of death row inmates. It's a standard feature of execution reporting. There've been books written on the subject. Galleries have exhibited the menus. We play a parlor game: what would you want if it were you?

Condemned prisoners often want diner food. Ricky Ray Rector, who murdered two people in Arkansas and then pretty much lobotomized himself with a gunshot to the head, requested steak, fried chicken, cherry Kool-Aid, and pecan pie. He ate it all, except the pie. The pie he left in his cell. Told the guard he was saving it for later. That prompted a last-minute appeal. Surely a man who's planning on pie when he gets back doesn't grasp what they're about to do to him. They executed him anyway.

In some prisons these days, the condemned no longer get to choose their last meals. It seems that too many dead men walking were ordering up sumptuous feasts, then just picking at them as the minutes ticked by. Now they're given the same thing as all the other prisoners, prison officials being mightily concerned about food waste and all.

Sometimes, sometimes when I'm at the Communion table eating the last meal Jesus ordered up before his own execution, I think about these things.

At the Table before Receiving

MARY LUTI

May we who are about to eat
the Last Meal of a doomed man
clamor and work to end the death penalty.
If we cannot or will not forgive,
at least let us not kill.
Amen.

Communion Is Not a Spiritual Experience

MARY LUTI

You cannot drink the cup of the Lord and the cup of demons. You cannot partake of the table of the Lord and the table of demons. (1 Corinthians 10:21, NRSV)

The Central African Republic (CAR) was once rife with anti-Muslim violence. Christians were the ones doing most of the killing. Politics was all tangled up in it, of course, but religious fervor drove the mayhem.

Christians didn't have a corner on that religious violence, of course. We still don't. Muslims bomb Christian churches, Hindus hunt down Buddhists, Buddhists terrorize Muslims, and just about everyone persecutes Jews.

Yet we Christians are the only ones who have Communion. Only Christians step over maimed bodies on our way to receive the Body of Christ. Only Christians can be found praying at the table, "Forgive us our trespasses as we forgive those who trespass against us." Only Christians exchange Christ's peace. Only Christians give each other bread with the words, "The Body of Christ." Only Christians extend our hands for that blessed bread, and say, "Amen." And only Christians claim at the same time that Communion is God's great "No" to violence.

You and I didn't murder Muslims in the CAR. But you don't have to kill or want to kill to make Communion a sham. You just have to receive the Body as if it has nothing to do with actual bodies. You just have to regard Communion as a "spiritual experience" untethered to earth and flesh. You just have to keep saying "Yes" to violence by what we do and leave undone, while in the broken bread Christ's God is screaming "No!"

Jesus gave us bread to eat, saying, "This is my body." He wasn't being spiritual. We commune with a human body that was tortured and slain.

We're meant to discern it, acknowledge it, consume it, and by our eating vow, "No more!"

Communion has many meanings, but in our violent days the sharing of bread at the Table of Love must at least be our way of declaring, "No more of this. One broken body was one too many."

No More of Death

—

LUKE 22:50-51; 1 CORINTHIANS 10:21
WORDS: **MARY LUTI**
MUSIC: **JODI HITZHUSEN**

No more of death:
Say no, say no, no more.
If here we're fed
with broken bread
we must say no, no more.

No harm and hate:
Say no, say no, no more.
If here we're filled
with lifeblood spilled
we must say no, no more.

No raging war:
Say no, say no, no more.
If here to each
we pass the peace
we must say no, no more.

No more of death:
Say no, say no, no more.
when tyrants press,
demanding yes,
we say, no more, no more.

—

Suggested use as a post-Communion sending hymn. The individual verses could also be interspersed with spoken prayers or affirmations, in call and response fashion. It may also be sung as a round.

No More of Death

Music by Jodi Hitzhusen
Lyrics by Mary Luti

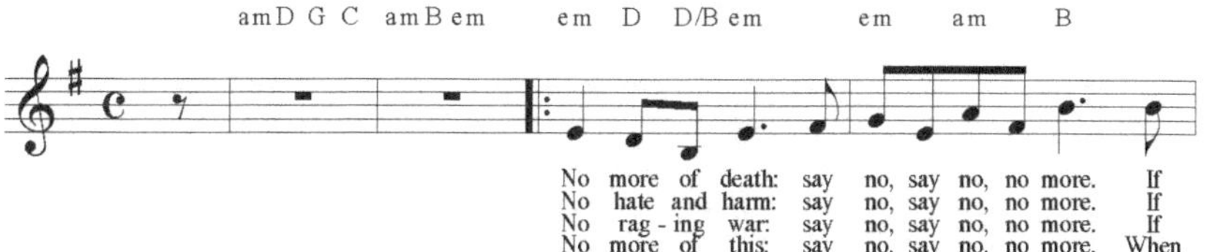

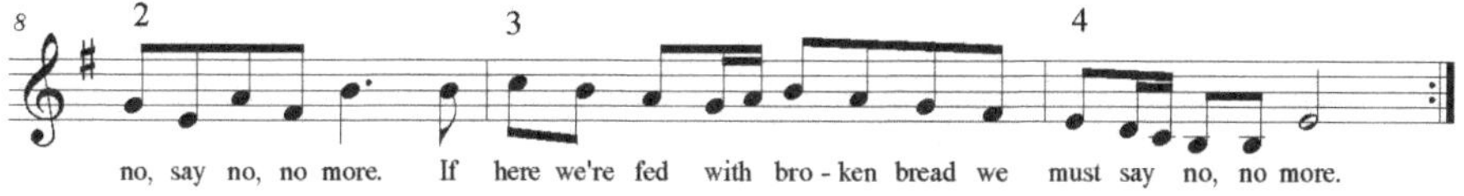

No More of This

CHRIS MERESCHUK

CONFESSION (LUKE 22:39-53, ABRIDGED)

In the Garden of Gethsemane, Jesus prayed:
"If you are willing, remove this cup from me;
yet, not my will but yours be done."
Jesus was in anguish, praying even more fervently.
His sweat became like drops of blood falling on the ground.
Judas arrived with a crowd, and betrayed Jesus with a kiss.
Those with Jesus were frightened, and asked him:
"Should we fight them with swords?"
Then one of them struck a servant, cutting off his ear.
But Jesus commanded: "No more of this!"
He touched the man's ear and healed him.

Let us pray:
Holy One, shed blood cries out to you —
sweat like drops of blood,
ice-cold blood of betrayal,
fiery blood fueled by anger and fear
causing blood on our swords,
blood on the body of the one who is cut open,
blood from the body of Jesus,
blood spilled from, on,
and by the Body of Christ.

But you do not demand this blood.
You cry out and say, "No more of this!"

Command us to stop the bloodshed.
Set your hand on us and heal us.
Cause our hands to drop our weapons.
Cause our mouths to cry out, "No more of this!"
And call our hearts to repentance.

SILENT CONFESSION

ASSURANCE OF GRACE

Sisters, Brothers, Siblings:
God has heard our confession.
God wills that we turn our hearts from violence,
our hands from harm to healing,
our ways from death to life.
Put your trust in the gospel of peace, and live!

REMEMBERING JESUS

Holy One, we praise you for all your gifts.
We remember your mercy towards us,
always calling us back to yourself
when we have fallen into the ways of violence.

And we remember with thanks your greatest gift to us,
your Child and our sibling, Jesus,
who suffered the violence we desire to renounce
with the help of your saving grace.

We remember that on the night he was handed over,
Jesus ate a meal with his disciples —
a celebration of a liberating covenant.
Among his friends at the table
was one who would deny him,
one who had already betrayed him,
and all who would abandon him.
And yet to each he gave the same blessing
and the same promise.
He never lost hope that we would learn his way.

And while they were eating,
he took bread from the table,
and after giving thanks, he divided it, saying:

"This is my body, broken for you."
This bread demands the end of broken bodies.
Take and eat it, everyone, and remember him.

Then he poured a cup and said:
"This cup is a new covenant in my blood."
This cup demands the end of bloodshed.
Take and drink it, everyone, and remember him.

BLESSING AND SENDING

May this foretaste of Heaven compel us all
to embody Christ's way of peace on earth,
proclaiming "No more of this!" to the violence of our world.

Do This, Not That

MARY LUTI

Then he took a loaf of bread, and when he had given thanks he broke it and gave it to them, saying, "This is my body, which is given for you. Do this in remembrance of me." And he did the same with the cup... (Luke 22:19-20, NRSVUE)

As a child, I was taught that Jesus died for our sins. We all deserved damnation because of them, but God willed that Jesus should be penalized instead. His death satisfied God's justice, and God extended to us again the friendship we'd lost, restoring harmony between heaven and earth.

"Substitutionary atonement" it's called, and for centuries most Western Christians have believed that it explains why Jesus had to die. Many have also adopted it as a pattern for dealing with societal fear and moral upset.

Whenever things go haywire, somebody must have done something wrong, somebody has to pay. So we find scapegoats and sacrifice them. It doesn't matter if they're innocent, just that they are blamed. God is placated, order is restored, peace reigns. At least for a while, anyway. Until we need to do it again. And again. Not to worry, 'though: there's no shortage of victims.

It's a simple, satisfying belief, as long as you don't mind that it makes God seem punishing, demanding piles of bodies to keep things on an even keel. Is there no other way to make amends, to establish peace, to set things right?

There is. It's right there in the story of the Last Supper. It's right there, at all our Communion tables. It's right there, if we want it: a substitutionary atonement without the bloodlust and the blasphemy.

Instead of a victim's body to shame and kill, Jesus substitutes bread to share and eat. Instead of innocent blood to spill, he substitutes wine to pour and drink. Instead of a righteous lynch mob, he substitutes humble fellowship. Instead of sacred violence, he substitutes a sacred meal. No more crosses, he says. Sit down instead. Bless bread. Pour wine. Eat and drink. Do this, not that.

---

*As suggested by S. Mark Heim, in *Saved from Sacrifice.*

NO ONE UNSATISFIED

Communion and Hunger

Bring It to Me

MARY LUTI

[The disciples] replied, "We have nothing here but five loaves and two fish." And [Jesus] said, "Bring them here to me." (Matthew 14:17-18, NRSV)

"But, Jesus," the disciples protest, "we have only this much food." They're doing triage, counting heads and fishes, tallying up loaves and mouths, making a plan—which is to stand there doing nothing, wringing their hands, because they can't make the numbers work.

Meanwhile, Jesus is thinking about the decisive nature of the little you have, the magnitude of small things, a mustard seed, a child in a manger, one coin lost in the house, one sheep detached from the fold, five small loaves, two fish.

He knows it takes a lot less than you think to satisfy the hunger you feel when you are down to nothing, nothing at all, in the larder of your heart.

It may be a miracle, but it isn't complicated. When the question is "With what?" you don't count to find the answer. You draw near. When the question is "But how?" the answer isn't plans and programs. It's proximity.

You have something? Anything? Just a little? Nothing at all? "Bring it here," Jesus says, "to me."

They did. And the rest is history. Well, not history exactly, but good news. That day, with Jesus so near, blessing their lack, everyone ate. This day, with Jesus so near, blessing your lack, you will, too. And some day, with all his disciples serving in proximity, so will the world.

Thousands on the Hillside

JOHN 6:1-13
WORDS: **MARY LUTI**
TUNE: **CRANHAM**
6.6.6.6.

Thousands on the hillside
Need that never ends
Empty of an answer
unprovisioned friends
Nothing but a child here
Only five small loaves
Two the fish for feeding
restless hungry droves

Large the crowd and craving
Small the hope inside
Large the question looming
Who can satisfy
Meager seems the offering
loving hands uplift
Large the grateful blessing
Greater still the gift

More than more remaining
more than food supplied
Dreams too small for dreaming
blessed and multiplied
Five small loaves a banquet
Two small fish increased
Take my little faith, Lord
Make my lack a feast

Every lack is plenty
Small is never small
By a grateful blessing

nothing turns to all
Great and mighty powers
tumble from their seat
Little ones are feasting
All the world is wheat

Suggested use as part of a liturgy of confession and assurance, or as a prayer of thanksgiving after Communion, or as a general Communion hymn.

Small Things

QUINN CALDWELL

Let's pray.

You gave us these jobs, O God:
remember, and tell.
And so we magnify you:

We remember that we have perceived you in small things:
nudges, flashes, suspicions, tastes, and hindsight.

We remember that we have found you in small things:
Bits of ancient writing,
single lines of music,
touch of gentle hands,
half-forgotten words.

We remember that you reveal yourself in one life:
One poor infant, one precocious child,
one young-adult voice, both beguiling and grating,
that invites the uninvited,
corrects the errant

gives purpose to the lost,
goads kings,
demands justice,
proclaims that today is the day,
and tells us to search for heaven
in the smallness of earth.

[The Lord's Prayer may be recited here.]

We remember a small group gathered in a small house.
A modest meal, an impossible claim:

That a loaf contains a life
and a cup holds a covenant.

We remember that we have tasted you in small things:
Cube, wafer, and morsel;
small glasses, tiny sips.

Too little for the already-sated
But for the hungry: enough.

So pour out your Holy Spirit—
still voice and rush of hurricane—
on these gifts, bread and drink and human,
carefully prepared, imperfectly offered.
Make them more:
turn smallness to sufficiency
bring largeness from lack
make imperfection enough.

Then let seed grow to fruits:
kindness and justice,
firmness and gentleness,
insight and bravery,
small voices amplified,
weak ones lifted,
the mighty made as small as you.
And then let a whole world spring
from the words we remember
we learned from you:
"Let there be..."
Amen.

Leftovers

MARY LUTI

For when the time comes to eat, each of you goes ahead with your own supper, and one goes hungry and another becomes drunk. (1 Corinthians 11:21, NRSV)

All ate and were filled; and they took up what was left over of the broken pieces, twelve baskets full. (Matthew 14:20, NRSV)

Years ago, a member of my congregation sidled up to me after Communion and cracked, "The service was great, but the portions were small." I laughed. And then I didn't.

So, let me ask, what's up with equal-sized portions, little cubes of precut bread, precisely measured thimblefuls of juice in identical, tiny cups? What's up with strict Communion parity, exactly this much and no more for everyone, precisely the same? Why couldn't Communion be more like a homemade meal at the family table where you can eat according to your hunger, according to your delight, just as much as you want or need?

St. Paul says that at the Lord's table no one should drink too much and get drunk or eat too little and starve. But that doesn't mean everyone should be served the same precisely pre-measured portions which, in case you hadn't noticed, always tend to be small.

Now, of course, Jesus can convey his loving presence to us by any means at all, including pristine half-inch square white bread cubes. His life will come to us abundantly even in shot glasses. That's nothing for him, he does it all the time. And sometimes, like during a pandemic, we have no choice but to use mass-produced, pre-proportioned containers, holy Keurig cups. It's necessary—the safe, prudent, and loving thing to do.

But when we have a choice?

When we have a choice, it's good to remember that Communion is a sign. It discloses God's generosity. It embodies God's unrestrained impulse to feed. It enacts divine justice, which is never minimal, but always maximal. With God, it's not just enough for all, it's always more than enough for anyone who needs more. If tiny Communion elements are any indication of what we think justice is, the one who collected twelve baskets of leftovers after the crowds ate as much as they wanted begs to differ.

Communities that get this will make sure there's abundant food for all. There will be leftovers. They'll gladly pass them around. Seconds and thirds for anyone who's still hungry.

We're always hungry. So hungry. Communities that get this will also give bread, wine, justice, and themselves to the world. In generous portions, with impeccable service, and even greater joy.

O Christ of Boundless Treasures

MATTHEW 14:13-21, MARK 6:30-44, LUKE 9:10-17, JOHN 6:1-15
WORDS: **MARY LUTI**
TUNES: **ANDÚJAR, WEST MAIN, WEDLOCK (AMERICAN/LOVELACE)**
7.6.7.6.D

O Christ of boundless treasures
in prodigal display,
all reckless like a spendthrift,
you give yourself away.
Yet we who claim to follow
prefer our portions small;
our timid calculation:
one little size for all.

No miracle of feeding
we offer crowds bereft;
no baskets for collecting,
no loaves and fishes left.
Withholding all your plenty,
we measure to each one
too little for the justice
that's begging to be done.

O Christ, in wasteful mercy,
come kindly and impart
in overflowing measure
the fullness of your heart;
then show us how to squander
the bread and wine of love,
dissatisfied forever
with barely just enough.

Suggested use as a confessional hymn, or as a general Communion hymn, or as a hymn to bless a feeding ministry.

No One Unsatisfied

MARILYN PAGÁN-BANKS

PRAYER OF CONFESSION

Abundant God, we say we believe in your provision,
yet we too often operate from a spirit of lack.
We lean on meritocracy—who is worthy or has earned what they get—
rather than trusting that you have created enough for all of us.
We demand equality rather than equity
because we don't want anyone to have more than us,
even if their need is greater.

Forgive us, God.
Stir up within us the joy of sufficiency and the delight
that comes in witnessing an empty plate and a smile
because all have had their fill.
We love you, Great Creator!
We are grateful for calling us to live generously.

APPROACHING THE TABLE

Jesus invites us to this holy meal with a spirit of abundance and hospitality. He doesn't want anyone going away unsatisfied, still feeling a gnawing emptiness. Jesus wants us to have our fill. It was out of this generous love that Jesus gathered with his followers on that Passover night long ago.

Imagine that there were more than the 12 in the room that night. Imagine it filled with women and children and others seeking to know more about Jesus. Even those that didn't believe, hanging around, lurking. Jesus, being who he was, would not have excluded anyone, not even his betrayer. Jesus, knowing God's promise, knew there would be more than enough for all.

Imagine the bread being passed not only around the table but also to those standing against the wall, sitting on the floor, gathered in the doorway. The cup quenching every thirst. No questions asked.

Imagine, and let us pray:

PRAYER OF THANKS

Holiest of Hosts, we give you thanks for your love and grace,
greater than we can hope for or imagine.
We thank you for your just and generous spirit
as we seek to embody it on this day as your church, your people.
We gather in thanksgiving,
God of provision and justice.
We gather in continual praise and worship,
God of joy and deliciousness, and we tell the old, old story.

TELLING THE STORY

On the night he was betrayed by one of his own,
before facing unlawful arrest and torture,
before beings executed by the state,
Jesus gathered with his disciples and the many that had followed him.

He took the bread, and 'though his heart was breaking,
he gave thanks to God.
He broke the bread and told them,
This is my body given for you, because I love you.
By the breaking of this bread,
may you find wholeness, healing, and fullness of life.
As often as you eat of this bread, re-member me.
Don't hold back. Tell the story.
Share my love. Feed my people. Be healed.

Then after supper, Jesus took the cup and said,
This is the cup of the new covenant.
A new promise, poured out freely for the forgiveness of sins,
and the restoring of our relationship with all creation.

As often as you drink this cup, re-member me.
Feel God's love course through your body
and allow it to flow out from you into a world
thirsty for love, kindness, forgiveness, and transformation.

PRAYER

God, we are grateful for these elements, bread and cup,
signs of your love, justice and grace.
As we partake in this feast today,
may we be transformed into this very love, justice, and grace made flesh
for the good of all creation.
Keep us ever thankful for your bountiful, steadfast care for us all.

INVITATION TO THE TABLE

Beloved, God invites you all by name.
We are all welcome to come and feast at Jesus' table
and to share in the joy of a common meal promising to fill us to overflowing.
Come and be transformed by the bread of life and the cup of the new covenant.
There is enough for us all, and more.
Come, all things are ready. *[The bread and cup are shared.]*

Love Lays a Splendid Table

WORDS: **MARY LUTI**
TUNES: **SALLEY GARDENS, NYLAND, MEIRIONYDD, WEDLOCK (AUSTIN LOVELACE)**
7.6.7.6.D

Love lays a splendid table
Love cannot be restrained
Love empties out its treasure
Love nothing has retained
Love lays a splendid table
Love feeds us every day
Love fashioned earth and heaven
Love gives it all away

Love lays a splendid table
Love nothing can withhold
Love serves the guests it gathers
Love doesn't need control
Love lays a splendid table
Love feeds us every day
Love fashioned earth and heaven
Love gives it all away

Love lays a splendid table
Love only wants to bless
Love casts aside its power
Love seeks to dispossess
Love lays a splendid table
Love feeds us every day
Love fashioned earth and heaven
Love gives it all away

Love lays a splendid table
Love lays down bread and bliss
Lay down yourself in loving

Love nothing asks but this
Love lays a splendid table
Love feeds us every day
Love fashioned earth and heaven
Love gives it all away

Suggested use as an invitation to the table or a general Communion hymn. The first lines may be sung by choir or soloist, and the chorus by the congregation.

Bread Alone

MARY LUTI

The tempter came and said to [Jesus], "If you are the Son of God, command these stones to become loaves of bread." But he answered, "It is written, 'One does not live by bread alone, but by every word that comes from the mouth of God.'" (Matthew 4:3-4, NRSV)

A famished Jesus was tempted by Satan in the wilderness, "Just turn these stones into bread!" But Jesus refused. "Human beings don't live by bread alone," he said, quoting scripture.

And it's true. Not all the nourishment we need for life is chewable. But that doesn't mean Jesus thought we should forego food. He fasted from time to time, but it wasn't his fasting that amazed his contemporaries. It was his indiscriminate eating with anyone who invited him. It was his feeding of multitudes.

He didn't turn those desert stones to bread; instead, he turned himself to living bread for everyone: love made food. His ministry was one long table. Wherever there's food, there's Jesus. Wherever Jesus is, there's food. Which is why we can count on him being truly present in Communion. There's so much hunger here, he can come to us only as bread.

A woman once approached Brazilian theologian Leonardo Boff after he finished the Mass. She said she'd received Communion unworthily that morning because she hadn't been to confession first, which was the rule. "I haven't eaten anything for three days," she explained, "and when I came in, you were handing out the wafers. So I ate one, because it's bread."

Because it's bread.

If feasting and feeding don't mark the church, if we don't always have food on our minds and in our hands, we haven't met Jesus. If the sharp hungers of our neighbors' bellies don't animate us, we've missed him and his meaning.

Given all the Suppers shared in our sanctuaries over the years, when there's even one person left in the world who's so hungry that a Communion wafer seems her only hope, everything about the church needs questioning. We're the ones who are eating unworthily at the table.

You Said that No One Lives by Bread

WORDS: **MARY LUTI**
TUNE: **SHEPHERDS' PIPES, KINGSFOLD**
8.6.8.6.D

You said that no one lives by bread,
by bread alone survives;
but by God's every Word of grace
the famished spirit thrives.
Yet in that empty wilderness
as pangs of hunger spread,
you also knew God's Word alone
can't take the place of bread.

We do not live by bread alone,
our spirits must be fed;
but there is so much hunger here:
O Jesus, give us bread!
A miracle of plenty now
in mercy still provide
to all who wait in aching hope
for justice multiplied.

We do not live by bread alone
but if you give us wheat,
we'll follow in your feeding way
until your work's complete.
Then lavish heaven will appear,
all hunger will have fled,
the world will feast on justice sweet,
and bread, and bread, and bread.

Suggested use as a hymn before Communion or as a general Communion hymn. It is especially apt for a worship service when a church's feeding ministry is being recognized.

Hungry, Fed, and Feeding

MATT LANEY

WELCOME

Are you hungry… for food, for love, for food that is love?
We are famished and longing for love.

Then this table is for you. Jesus is for you.
Wherever there's food, there's Jesus.
Wherever Jesus is, there's food.
Are we worthy of it?

If you are hungry, you are worthy. Come and find what you need.

PRAYER OF THANKS AND PRAISE

Let us pray:
Gracious God, our Host,
we come humbly, hungrily, maybe hangrily,
for food that fills and fulfills.
Here you meet us not only as server, but also as the serving,
not only as baker, but also as the bread.
We sit at your table, grateful, eager,
wondering if this is too good to be true.

We are like those who gathered at a table long ago
on the night Jesus was arrested and taken away.
He sat with his companions to enjoy a Passover meal.
They re-told the story of your liberating love.
They sang the ancient hymns and ate the ritual meal.
And still they hungered, for love, for justice,
for healing, pardon and peace.

So Jesus took bread, blessed it and broke it.
He shared it with them saying,
"This bread is me, my own body, given for you.
Take and eat to remember me."

He also took his cup, filled it with wine, and blessed it, giving thanks.
He shared it with them saying, "This is the cup of a new covenant, my blood, my life.
Drink it to remember me."

PRAYER TO THE HOLY SPIRIT

**Generous One,
pour out your Spirit on this food and drink.
Make them for us the very presence of Jesus,
so that as we receive and share them,
we receive and share him.**

INVITATION TO THE TABLE

All who hunger are worthy and welcome
to share in the gifts of Jesus' table,
whether you are hesitant or not, believe a little or believe a lot.
This food is for you.

THANKSGIVING AFTER COMMUNION

**Host of hosts, receiving Jesus at his table means
keeping food on our minds and in our hands.
Well-fed and grateful, send us into the world
that waits in aching hope for bread and justice multiplied,
ready to serve, and forever praising your name.**

Don't Disappoint Melanie

MARY LUTI

They said, "It is written, '[God] gave them bread from heaven to eat.'" … Jesus said, "I am the bread…" (John 6:31, 35, NRSV)

During a class on the sacraments, a student, Carol, told this story: After a snowstorm, only a few folks who lived within trudging distance made it to church, including Carol and her daughter, Melanie, who was four. The service was simple: a hymn, scripture, Communion.

Melanie had never received Communion, but she was there, and no one was stopping her, so she held out her hand. With everybody else in the reverent circle, she ate. Then she broke the hush:

"Mommy!" she cried, "This is the most delicious bread!"

Adults overthink everything. Especially Communion. We divide into theological camps over it. We exclude people deemed morally, denominationally, doctrinally unfit. We bar little children until they're capable of abstraction. We understand everything about bread except that you're meant to eat it.

But Melanie tasted what we forget—before all else, Communion is food, delectable Presence, Jesus' sweet-surrendered self. It is the most delicious Bread.

You don't need to be grown-up or confirmed to know that something tastes good; to savor a grace of exceptional flavor; to sense that this is a mercy and no ordinary thing; to be surprised at it, grateful; to cry out, delighted. You need only be there, extending your hand. You need only eat.

And so, by the way, if Communion isn't delicious in your church, if it's gummy Wonder white or sawdust gluten-free, why not replace it with something less disagreeable? It's hard to believe you're at heaven's feast when the meal tastes like cardboard and glue. When choosing an edible sign that Christ is truly with us, always go for flavor. Do not disappoint Melanie.

And don't disappoint the world that needs us, who eat the bread, to be more than a thin starchy presence for the hunger of bodies and souls. The world that needs us, who drink the cup, to spill out onto its thirst a love more generous than a thimble cup. That needs us, who have known the meal's delight, to be delicious.

Most Delicious Bread

WORDS: **MARY LUTI**
TUNES: **FOREST GREEN, KINGSFOLD, SALVATION (BOYD)**
8.6.8.6.D

O Christ, you knead your love for us
in most delicious bread,
with milk and honey, yeast and salt,
the tastes of heaven wed;
and even little ones enjoy
the flavor of your wheat
and join the circle of your guests
at mercy's welcome seat.

Communion's mystery is deep,
there's much to learn and teach,
but knowledge cannot satisfy
and theories cannot reach
the cravings of a hungry heart
for most delicious bread,
the warm and fragrant gift of you
at heaven's lavish spread.

Make us like you, a honeyed loaf
to answer hunger's cry.
The hope of people everywhere
knead us to satisfy.
No ordinary gift we'll give,
as all are justly fed,
but pure delight, uncommon love:
the most delicious bread.

Suggested use as a hymn before Communion is served, or as a special blessing of the congregation's bread makers or of its meal ministry.

Most Delicious Bread

RACHEL HACKENBERG

INVITATION

A feast! A delight for our tongues,
a joy for our spirits, an extravagance for our bodies!
What revelations will we understand
if we truly stop to savor the gifts of the table?
What hungers will be satisfied if we take our time
to appreciate the earthiness of yeast and the sweet flesh of grapes?
In response to Christ's beckoning, let us find out.

PRAISE AND THANKSGIVING

Welcome to Christ's table.
We are glad to be here!
Lift up your hunger.
We do not hide our needs before God.
Prepare yourself to be hosted and fed.
The Bread of Life is our joy and satisfaction.

Most Holy Sustenance,
we praise you for creation and its fruits, for labor and its harvest.
What a miracle it is to taste and know the holiness of life!
What a mercy it is to hunger and be satisfied!
You have put a grain of salt on our tongues so we might relish you.
You have called us salt of the earth so we might relish one another.

When the way is hard, you pour out honey.
When our souls are weary, you overflow with milk.
We gratefully return to your feast at this table,
trusting you will meet and feed us again
with the love that is a fragrant zest in the air.

The feast is holy because you are God Most Holy.
The banquet is appetizing because the Spirit calls us here.
And the company is a blessing because Jesus loves each one of us.

SHARING THE MEAL

[The story of the Last Supper may be retold, and then the elements are consecrated.]

Bless this grain, bless this fruit,
and bless those who eat
with the outpouring of the Holy Spirit.
We ask this in the name of Jesus, Bread of Life,
who taught us to pray.

[The Lord's Prayer may be said.]

Come and know.
Taste and see.
Savor and be glad.
In the bread and in the cup,
find the deliciousness of Christ, who is our life.
This is the feast of God for all people.

POST-COMMUNION PRAYER

Most Delicious Bread,
once again you have satisfied us
and we are thankful.
In the spirit of fullness,
make us generous with one another.
In the hope of all people being fed,
make us salt and yeast in the world. Amen.

YOU GIVE THEM SOMETHING TO EAT

Communion and Just Mercy

The Church Has Bread

MARY LUTI

The disciples said, "Send the crowds away, so they can go buy themselves some food." Jesus replied, "You give them something to eat." (Matthew 14:13-16, abridged)

It used to be that if you didn't understand it, weren't baptized, didn't believe correctly, or weren't considered morally pure, you were barred from Communion. It was called "fencing the table." Everybody did it.

But these days some churches are unfencing. Completely. They say Jesus never turned anyone away from his table, so neither should we.

Never mind that Jesus was always a guest with no table of his own to welcome anyone to. Or that early on, the church began emphatically excluding notorious sinners, the unbaptized, and heretics. Or that the church has consistently taught that Communion is for members only.

We're opening our tables anyway, even 'though we've never done it this way before. And now many people once ruled out are coming. Little kids, unbaptized adults, intellectually disabled people, the weary, the sin-sick, the wary, the doubting, the curious—they're all coming.

Because they want it, this gift they can't explain, don't believe in correctly, or were told they don't deserve. They want it, this company for their loneliness, this healing for their estrangement, this home for their wandering, this approval for their very beings. This pardon. This love. This memory. This meeting. This mercy. This food.

Above all, this food. For a bottomless hunger.

And the church that's always needed to have all its theological ducks in a row before budging an inch; the church that's always gone to the wall for its beliefs and put others up against the wall for theirs; this obtuse yet still teachable church is finally starting to obey Jesus: "You give them something to eat."

There is so much hunger.

The church has bread.

Open Table

WORDS: **MARY LUTI**
TUNES: **WEST MAIN, HEAVENLY ARMOUR (SOUTHERN HARMONY)**
7.6.7.6.D

You don't have to be perfect
You don't have to be pure
You don't have to be righteous
You don't have to be sure
You just need to be hungry
You just need to be fed
You just need heaven's manna
You need to need the Bread

So Jesus says, Come eat here,
whoever you may be
His bread is for the taking
for you, and even me
No questions will be asked here
no test will be applied
The only thing you need is
a need to satisfy

You don't have to have answers
You don't have to impress
You don't have to be certain
You don't have to confess
You just need to be thirsty
You just need filling up
You just need heaven's fountain
You need to need the Cup

So Jesus says, Come drink here,
whoever you may be
His cup is for the taking
for you, and even me

No questions will be asked here
no test will be applied
The only thing you need is
a need to satisfy

Suggested use as an invitation to the table, either at the start of the Communion liturgy or immediately before Communion is served.

Table or Not

PHIWA LANGENI

INVITATION

Whether there are 13 people gathered on one side of one long table,
or 56 grouped around tables in the fellowship room,
the invitation remains:
We are called and welcomed to satisfy our hunger.

Whether there are 5,000 people on a hillside eating from their laps,
or 1 on a couch in the living room eating from a TV table,
the invitation remains:
We are called and welcomed to satisfy our thirst.

Whether there are 20 people bumping elbows in a dining hall,
or 6 squatting hip-to-hip around a shared bowl,
the invitation remains:
We are called and welcomed to satisfy our need for the Bread.

Whether we find ourselves at literal tables of various shapes,
or at some of the many other ways we gather to eat,
the invitation remains:
We are called and welcomed to satisfy our need for the Cup.

REMEMBRANCE

We are invited, once again, to come feast at this sacred table.
And as we do, we remember that final gathering
at that familiar table with Jesus and his friends.

That night started out like many others before
as they shared stories along with the bread and cup,
filling their spirits and bodies with a communal meal.

But this night was different.
Aware of the betrayal that would lead to his death,
Jesus drew meaning from their meal-sharing
so that they – and we! – would always
remember, even after he was gone.
He took that basic bread, blessed and broke it, saying,
"This is my body, shared with you.
Every time y'all do this, remember."

And after they supped,
Jesus blessed and poured that common cup,
saying,
"This is the cup of the new covenant, poured for you.
Every time y'all do this, remember."
In this very hour,
we remember: Jesus invites everyone, table or not.

In this very hour,
we remember: the Church has bread, table or not.

In this very hour,
we remember: all we need is to need the Bread and Cup, table or not.

INVOCATION OF THE SPIRIT

Let us invite the Spirit to visit this meal.

Infuse yourself into each element, Holy One,
so that we can encounter you wholly as one.
When we eat and drink,
give us the wisdom to celebrate
and the courage to embody
the diverse grains and droplets
that form this sacred meal.

Make us grateful for all we are about to receive
and unite us in love, now and always. Amen.

INVITATION

Come and eat. Table or not, all things have been made ready.

THANKSGIVING

Let us pray.
Thank you, Maker and Breaker of Tables,
for inviting me—and us all!—
to partake in this sacred meal.
Even as we have gotten our fill today,
keep our hungers unsatisfied
and our thirsts unquenched
so that we might do and be the Church,
always in remembrance of you. Amen.

Wide Mercy, Wide Table

DONNA SCHAPER

Holy One, we know that your table
is not in a restaurant or in a home.
It's in a church.
We know that sacred space is different,
mostly because of the way
your Holy Spirit visits us in it.
Beckon that Spirit to us now.
Let us imagine and know
that we are seated here
with our enemies, our friends,
people we don't know,
people who are gone from our lives,
even newcomers,
the kind that migrate from far away worlds.
Let this table be so wide that we start humming,
"There's a wideness in your mercy,
like the wideness of the sea."

Come, Jesus Calls to Near and Far Away

WORDS: **MARY LUTI**
TUNE: **A VA DE**
10.10.10.10

Come, Jesus calls to near and far away
Come, Jesus wants to feed us all today
Sets a place for every hurting sad one
And a place for every joyous glad one

Come, Jesus lays aside his majesty
Come, Jesus serves us all on bended knee
No one low or high, no least or greatest
He will feed alike the first and latest

Come, Jesus gives himself, a holy sign
Come, Jesus offers us good bread and wine
Heals the sad divisions we are harmed by
Everyone's the apple of his love's eye

Come, Jesus calls us all to be his friends
Come, Jesus tends to us so we can tend
Death-defying ministry he's giving
Grace poured out on everything that's living

Suggested use as an invitation to the table. It can be sung in a call-and-response style, with a leader singing the first two lines of each stanza, and the congregation coming in to complete the verse.

You Have Set Your Table Wide

MARY LUTI

O Jesus, you have set your table wide
with welcome every creature longs to find;
so we have come to drink the cup of joy
and eat with thanks the bread of life you give.

But first we must confess with humble hearts
the anxious fears that contradict this sign,
that there won't be enough for everyone,
and we alone deserve the most, and more.

How easily our hearts believe the lie
that status, wealth, and power have the right
to corner all the wondrous gifts of life,
to clean the plate and leave no crumb behind.

Have mercy, Jesus, medicine and life!
Restrain and heal our unchecked appetites.
Help us forsake the grasping way we live,
our dashing to the front of every line.

At life's abundant banquet give us light
to notice empty chairs and plates unfilled,
the silent spaces haste and greed create,
and, grieving, pledge to wonder, work, and wait.

Then will Communion be a faithful sign
unveiling you, O Jesus, just and good;
then, only then, we'll eat your Supper true,
and only then, in honest praises, pray. Amen.

Mercy Me

DONNA SCHAPER

O God, today we remember
the way the old folk say, "Mercy me,"
and indicate by their tone of voice,
by their shock and amazement,
their willingness to be surprised over and over.
Visit us with the power of your Holy Spirit
in this bread and wine.
Fill us with your grace
so that we can mercy ourselves
and mercy each other all day long,
this day and maybe even tomorrow. Amen.

Distributing Jesus

MARY LUTI

While they were eating, Jesus took a loaf of bread, and after blessing it he broke it, and gave it to [them]. (Matthew 26:26, NRSV)

We imagine Jesus handing a loaf down the table, disciple to disciple. But scripture says only that he gave it to them, so we don't really know how it got distributed. But we do know how we give out Communion—in lots of different ways.

We approach the server, we're given bread, we dip it in the cup and eat. We kneel at a rail, and the server brings the bread and the cup to us. We sit in pews, passing plates of bread and rattling trays of little glasses. We prefer some methods to others, sometimes ferociously; yet we manage to find devotional meaning in them all, attaching symbolism to going forward, kneeling, or passing the elements to each other in the pews.

But we don't really need to invent meanings for our various ways of getting Communion off the table and into our hands. All these methods are already meaningful just by being what they are—practicalities, efficiencies, delivery systems. For no matter the method we employ, the Spirit is training us in a vital Christian competence: the skill of distribution. We're practicing God's own resourcefulness in providing food to every living thing.

Next time you take canned goods to the food bank, organize meals at the shelter, set supper on your family's table, pass out sandwiches to unhoused people in the park, or lobby for food justice in the halls of power, remember going forward to be given bread. Remember the server at the rail. Remember trays of little glasses passed in pews. Remember that Jesus "gave it to them." And be awed by what a holy thing it is to distribute food.

O Christ, We Gladly Offer You

WORDS: **MARY LUTI**
TUNE: **FOREST GREEN**
8.6.8.6.D

O Christ, we gladly offer you
to all who wait and pray
at kneeling rails, in moving lines,
in chairs, or passing trays.
Our open hearts accept your gift
however it may come,
distributed by many means
to each and every one.

For you intend that all receive
the love this gift conveys.
You humbly bow to human need
and honor human ways,
content by any means we use
to come to us and stay,
as long as all are fed and blessed
and no one's turned away.

And so by practices diverse
your church acquires the art
of distribution past its walls
to every hungry heart
in food banks, soup lines, on the streets;
while loudly we demand
the right to food for everyone,
obeying love's command.

So we will offer you to all
by every means we know,
not fretting over how to serve,
but by our serving show

how eagerly you seek our hearts,
how varied your embrace,
how indiscriminate your love,
your vast unfussy grace.

Suggested use as a teaching hymn—for example, during a deacons' or Communion servers' retreat/training, or when a new distribution method is being introduced to the congregation—as a celebration hymn of the congregation's ministry, or as a general hymn for Communion.

In Many Different Ways

MARY LUTI

INVITATION, THANKS AND PRAISE

In how many ways does God come to us?
Balm in sorrow
Encouragement in trouble
Joy in joy
Strength in struggle
Perseverance in challenge
Light in shadow
Healing in pain
Mercy for shame
Mother, Father
Life and love
Always love

Praise to God forever!

In how many ways does Jesus come to us?
Teacher
Prophet
Wonder worker
Company in loneliness
Refreshment in wilderness
Bracing truth
Resilient life
Hope when hope was gone
Meal maker
Feeder
Befriender
Feasting friend

Praise to God forever!

What can keep Christ's love from us?

Not authorities and powers
Not locked doors in rooms where we're hiding
Not unbelief, or wrong belief, or belief itself
Not the shape of our bodies
Not our race or culture
Not our abilities or disabilities
Not our genders or identities
Not our money or lack of money
Not our fear
Not out pride in righteousness
Not our sins
Never our sins
Not even the grave

Praise to God forever!

Loving Presence comes to us
in ways too many to count.
Love arrives however it can.
Our unfussy Giver gives inventively,
flexibly, freely, ingeniously,
unstymied by obstacles,
unbound by convention and rules,
in new ways, old ways, any way at all,
as long as it works,
as long as Mercy gets distributed abundantly,
to us, to them, to everyone.

Praise to God forever!

REMEMBERING JESUS

Now with grateful hearts, let us pray:
Feed us now, Holy One, in whatever way works.
Help us remember the feeding hands of Jesus
and all the ways he distributed your food to us
on hillsides, in upper rooms, on lakeshores,
and in Emmaus, the evening of his rising.

He always found a way to reach us with mercy,
to nourish us with love. We never went without.

Even on the night of betrayal
he divided the bread he blessed
and gave it to us, handing us also the cup,
brimful and blessed— naming them signs of his self-gift,
the real presence of an embodied love
stronger than the death we would deal him.

Now at this table we do again
what he asked us to do that night:
remember him by blessing and sharing,
by finding a way to feed.

With thanks, we eat and drink
so that we may become one Body in love
with one Lifeblood coursing through us,
carrying on one ministry:
to give God's gifts away
in any way we can devise,
in every way we can devise,
to every child of God.

SHARING BREAD AND CUP

These are God's gifts for God's people.
Let's practice now the holy skill of distribution,
giving them to one another generously, with joy and thanks.

THANKSGIVING

Let us pray:

Thank you for giving yourself to us
in so many different ways.
May we too distribute you to all
in new ways, old ways, every way, any way,

so that the hungry will be fed,
the dying will have life,
the lonely will be accompanied,
the oppressed will have justice,
and all of us together
will rejoice in your love.
In Jesus' name we pray. Amen.

Communion's Politics

MARY LUTI

Do you want to honor Christ's body? Then do not honor him in church while neglecting him outside where he is cold and naked. For he who said: "This is my body," also said: "You saw me hungry and did not feed me." (St. John Chrysostom)

I once read that the hungry poor of the Brazilian Northeast avoid eating in front of others. It shames them to display the bottomless pit of their need in public. For them, eating is private, like sex and defecation.

Think about that: hungry people always eating the little they have out of sight, their world reduced, their lives shrunk. It's atomizing. It makes social solidarity impossible.

Now think about Communion: a table where everyone may come and eat equally in full view of the world, the very picture of social solidarity.

In a world constructed to starve many so that a few can overeat, a world designed to destroy human bonds, to atomize by shame, Communion is a political manifesto. Listen to our scriptures:

Paul denounces the Corinthians for excluding the hungry poor from the Supper. To eat the Meal but offer no communal response to hunger nullifies Holy Communion. And human communion.

Mary's "Magnificat" announces that in God's world the rich relinquish their advantages and the poor are well fed. The table is the reverse image of the world's economics.

Jesus teaches his disciples to ask, "Give us this day our daily bread." Not me and my bread, but us and ours. Concern for others' bread is the Christian's marching orders.

For centuries, we Christians have argued over what happens when someone says holy words over bread and wine. But while people are starving, we might better ask what could happen if we'd raise Communion's ethical fist to make sure they're fed.

This, My Body, Blessed and Given

WORDS: **MARY LUTI**
TUNE: **FORTUNATUS NEW**
8.7.8.7.8.7

This, my body, blessed and given,
starving, naked, left for dead.
Needing a meal, a hand, a neighbor,
peace for never-ending dread.
You in church here, fed and singing,
won't you share with me my bread?

This, my body, blessed and given,
long denied a crumb, a shred.
Hoping for hope, and somehow dreaming,
hanging by a slender thread.
You in church here, fed and singing,
won't you share with me my bread?

This, my body, blessed and given,
passed to you with joyful care.
'Round this table, words of glory,
'round the world, tears of despair.
You in church here, fed and singing,
share my bread with me out there.

Suggested use during a time of confession and assurance before Communion, or as part of a post-Communion sending.

Hungry

DONNA SCHAPER

As we bring your bread to our lips today, O Christ,
may we remember someone who has none
and will have none tomorrow and had none yesterday.

As we lift your cup to our lips today, O Christ,
may we remember someone who has never known joy,
who has no glass or friend with whom to drink from a glass.

When we say a prayer of thanksgiving at the end of this Meal—
the meal that promises someday everyone will eat,
everyone will rejoice, and all will be well—
when we close out today with "Thank you,"
let us tremble when we whisper it.

Thank you.
Amen.

EATING OUR WAY TO LOVE

Communion and Reconciliation

Is It I, Lord?

MARY LUTI

As they were eating, [Jesus] said, 'Truly I say to you, one of you will betray me." They were sorrowful and began to say to him one after another, "Is it I, Lord?" (Matthew 26:21-22, ESV)

At Communion, pastors often point out that a betrayer, a denier, and several deserters ate with Jesus that last night. If he welcomed them, he'll surely welcome us. Which is true, and good news for all.

But if the presence of sinners at Jesus' table serves only to reassure us of our worthiness and welcome, we whitewash the church's memory, glossing over the unsettling scene of a troubled Jesus repeatedly disrupting the evening's camaraderie to indict his friends: "You will all become deserters." "One of you will betray me." "Before morning, you will deny me."

He didn't say those things for welcome's sake. He called them out publicly so that there could be truth in the room. Jesus had eagerly desired to eat the feast with his friends. But he wasn't about to eat it in denial. Neither should we.

No denial: U.S. mainline Protestant congregations are overwhelmingly White, and not by accident. Many congregations refuse to face what that means. We who celebrate Communion in White-dominant churches speak easily of the Body's wholeness, even as our demographics at the table dismember it. Racism eats with us every time we bless and share Christ's bread. Few of us ask, "Is it I?"

Not all was well as Jesus' table. He said so. Not all is well at ours. Let's not pretend. Instead of remembering Jesus in ways that always reassure us, let's also remember him in ways that call us out, unmask the denial in our mantras of inclusion, and compel us to address the trauma in Christ's Body with the truth, and nothing but.

What We Have Done

MARY LUTI
TUNE: **PROSPECT (GRAHAM), DISTRESS, BOURBON, WHEN JESUS WEPT**
8.8.8.8

What we have done, how can it mend?
What we have done, when will it end?
What we have done, can all be well?
Will no one tell what we have done?

What we have done, uncover here.
What we have done, let truth appear.
What we have done let Love reveal,
that Love might heal what we have done.

Here humbly sit at Mercy's spread.
With broken hearts lift broken bread.
Pour Pardon's cup and let tears fall,
remembering all that God has done.

Suggested use as a confession before Communion during a racial justice-themed worship service or at any Communion service in a White-dominant congregation that has undertaken a serious grappling with racism.

Holy Accountability for Racism

LIZ MILLER

PRAYER OF CONFESSION

O God, who in the same breath calls us into community and calls out injustice: we are not well.

For too long your vision for a church free from oppression has been just that: a far-off vision, a someday dream, a hope that we long for but are unable to embody.

We make excuses for our past sins while refusing to hold our present selves accountable.

We hide behind good intentions instead of exposing the impact of our actions.

We settle for a status quo that privileges whiteness even as we wonder why Sunday morning remains the most segregated hour in America.

In listening to Jesus' hard truths spoken to betrayers and deniers, may we hear his call to us:

A call to look within at the prejudices we have inherited from the communion of saints.

A call to reject the systems and practices that enforce racism inside and outside the church.

A call to cast aside the idol of white supremacy that prevents the body of Christ from reconciling with itself.

Even when we get it wrong, even when we stumble or fail, may we hear your sacred voice of accountability, calling us back again, and again, and again.

Hear these words, not as a hall pass to continue to harm one another, but to give us the courage to do better: you are beloved by God and in Christ you are forgiven.

May we be known as people of reconciliation and grace! Thanks be to God!

Partners

MARY LUTI

They devoted themselves to the apostles' teaching and to fellowship, to the breaking of bread and to prayer... They [all] ate together with glad and sincere hearts. (Acts 2:42 & 46, NIV)

Two deacons intensely disliked each other. Everybody dreaded deacons' meetings because of the way those two went at it. Even the church's new behavioral covenant didn't stop them. It was bad.

That same church had weekly Communion, and it was the deacons' job to serve the congregation. This they did in pairs, according to a predetermined schedule. It was also customary that when each pair finished serving all the people who came to their station, they turned and served each other.

The two warring deacons were never paired up on the schedule. The head deacon worried that partnering them would lead to fireworks. But one Sunday morning during Communion, she had an epiphany. That afternoon she made a new schedule, assigning the enemies to each other. For six months.

They were shocked and unhappy, but they bit their tongues and went along. Thus it was that every week they turned to each other and said: "The bread of life, for you." Every week: "The cup of blessing, for you." Every week for months: "Amen."

I'd like to say they became great friends. They didn't. Communion isn't magic. Still, you can't offer mercy to an enemy every week and not start to mean it, even a little. You can't put healing into someone's hand for months on end without something rubbing off.

Something did. Their disagreements felt less wounding. Occasionally they'd defer to each other. And when the six months ended and they got new partners, they seemed to some of us to be a bit bereft.

O Christ, We Cannot Cling for Long

WORDS: **MARY LUTI**
TUNES: **KINGSFOLD, STAR OF THE COUNTY DOWN, TUOLUMNE, FOREST GREEN**
8.6.8.6.D

O Christ, we cannot cling for long
to bitterness and strife
with those to whom we turn and say,
"For you, the Bread of Life!"
And we cannot refuse for long
a pardoning embrace
to anyone we serve and say,
"For you, the Cup of Grace!"

And so into each waiting hand
we place your mercy bread
and pass it 'round and 'round until
with pardon all are fed.
And into every outstretched hand
we place your healing cup
and pass it round and round until
we bind each other up.

O reconciling Christ, we pray
by gifts of wine and bread
relieve our anger-laden hearts
and give us joy instead;
and in good time and by your grace,
with every drop and crumb
remake us, partners of your love,
your peaceful kingdom come.

Suggested use: As a general hymn for Communion, underlining the reconciling work of Christ at the table. As a confession and assurance before Communion. Or in a retreat setting where Communion is served informally, hand to hand, to strengthen the "ties that bind in Christian love."

In the Presence of My Enemies

MOLLY PHINNEY BASKETTE

You prepare a table before me in the presence of my enemies. You anoint my head with oil. My cup runneth over. (Psalm 23:5, NRSV)

In seminary, I did a summer of chaplaincy training in a juvenile detention facility. At the end of my time, as a way of saying goodbye to the teens I'd grown very close to, I shared with them an agape meal of good bread and grape juice.

One of the guards, who was unnecessarily sarcastic and strict and with whom I'd been tangling all summer, was on duty and stood off to the side.

I knew what I had to do. And I didn't want to do it.

Wasn't this the enemy of the kids I loved? Condemning them, in my mind, to a lifetime of being society's convenient scapegoats in the school-to-prison pipeline? How dare God nudge me to include him in this feast? He didn't deserve it, and inviting him might do more harm than good to the youth—especially if he rejected the invitation.

But we ignore God's invitation to reconciliation, true communion, at our peril. I turned and faced him. "Would you like to join us?"

All the boys watched to see what would happen. He came and stood with us in our tight circle, and they made space for him. I gave the instructions for intinction and how to pass the elements. I told them that this was holy food. To take it was to claim one's rightful place in the family of God, as children of God. To offer it to the person next to them was to affirm that they, too, were a beloved child of God, free in the deepest sense.

The boys were uncharacteristically solemn during the ritual. And the guard received the cup from the boy on his right, he didn't dip his bread in it as the others had. He tipped it back and drank directly from it. He drank directly from the cup that all those young hands had just grazed.

The cup is a symbol of shared fate. Jesus said to the disciples, knowing he himself was about to become a scapegoat for society's sins, "Can you drink this cup that I am about to drink?" He was asking, "Are you willing to become powerless and suffer as I will?"

The disciples answered, "We are able."

I don't know where those boys or that guard are today. I'm not naive enough to think it changed the course of any of their lives. But maybe, just maybe, that simple sip, shared spit, shared suffering, shared siblinghood in the Kin-dom of God, opened a previously locked door.

Reconciliation

MOLLY PHINNEY BASKETTE

INVITATION

The psalmist sang,
"You prepare a table for me in the presence of my enemies."

This is not a taunting meal with Usses and Thems.
It's a place, a time when even enemies can feast together.

Come, then, you who have harsh words between you.
Stand side by side in silence.

Come, you who have fought good fights and bad fights and everything in between.
Find peace, if only for a moment.

Come, you who can't yet face each other fully.
Find the face of God in every sibling.

God abhors abuse, and never asks us to submit to the domineering strength of another.
But true reconciliation among people on equal footing sets us free and transforms conflict into amazing grace.

So lay aside argument, distance, alienation,
confusion, power over, and even principles.
Come to this feast empty, hungry, and ready.

PRAYER OF CONSECRATION

Holy One, you inhabit these elements of bread and cup.
As each has already been transformed
from what it was into something more nourishing,
ready to give energy to the body,

so transform us into those who can nourish the world.
As we pull from a common loaf, unite us.
As we drink from a common cup, a symbol of shared fate,
send us down the same road, with strength in numbers.
Make us truly one in Christ.

BREAD AND CUP

We remember that on the night before he died,
Jesus sat at table with all of them: friend and foe.
He didn't ask how they had voted,
where they stood on church doctrines,
or whether they would remain true, even to him.

He took bread, and giving thanks to God, he said to all,
"Take, eat, this is my body, given for you. Do this and remember me."

He took wine and said,
"This is not just a cup—it's a covenant, to bind us together,
to help us forget the sins of the past."

Ministering to you in the name of Jesus, the Great Uniter, we partake of this feast.

THANKSGIVING

God, let the unity we have at this table endure
long after we have digested these elements.
Feed our minds the manna of gentleness
and the ability to take another's perspective.
Juice us with the joy that comes when we can set aside our differences
and come together as your children.
Thank you that every time we eat this meal together,
you give us an opportunity to lay down arms, stop taking sides,
and find again our common humanity and divinity. Amen.

Needing to Eat

MARY LUTI

When they had gone ashore, they saw a charcoal fire there, with fish on it, and bread... Jesus said to them, "Come and have breakfast." (John 21:9, 12, NRSV)

A family trip to Italy. We'd spent the day in Gubbio, where St. Francis befriended a ravenous wolf who was killing livestock and people. The terrified townsfolk wanted him dead. Francis proposed a mutual-aid pact. The wolf would stop killing, and the people would feed him. Peace reigned.

My Uncle Dick is no St. Francis. He's disturbed the peace all day, your basic ugly American. By the time we get back to our rented villa, we'd rather drink battery acid than spend another minute together.

But we're hungry. We need to eat.

We drift to the kitchen, avoid eye contact, rummage through the fridge, head for the table outside. I bring the bread, Dad the wine, Phyllis fruit and walnuts, Chick brined artichokes and cold pork. Dick arrives last, points to the spread, and says, "Ciao!" For some reason, we find this hilarious.

We eat. The sun sets. Stars come out. We're still eating. Chick tells racy stories about her first boyfriend. We harmonize, "Baby, It's Cold Outside." By midnight we've polished off everything but the walnuts. Someone starts "Good Night, Irene." We push back our chairs and go to bed. So full, and not just from the food.

To understand Communion, you could study theology. But you could also just share a meal. Even with family dinners going the way of the dinosaur, we know that the chances of loving each other increase when we eat together. Surprising things happen at tables, especially if we aren't too choosy about our companions. Surprising things like healing, pardon, and peace.

Because some meals are so good, they can make you laugh at an irritating uncle's stupid joke. Some so fine and plentiful we'd wish them for everyone, even a betrayer. Some are garnished with songs so sweet, stories so compelling, and stars so bright they make you remember the good you'd forgotten and forget the bad you thought you'd never survive. For a moment, anyway, it seems possible to forgive just about anything. And you think, "So this is the way it was meant to be!"

When you really need to eat, Communion is food. It's company, miraculously dear. It's a story told till the sun goes down. An old song sung till the stars come out. It's pardon, healing, and heart-swelling peace. It's life eternal in the dawning day.

Weary Souls and Tiresome Friends

WORDS: **MARY LUTI**
TUNE: **FALCONE (CAROL DORAN)**
7.7.7.7.D

Weary souls and tiresome friends,
strangers raising vague alarm,
loved ones meaning no offense,
carelessly inflicting harm;
enemies fixed on the past,
still unwilling to retreat;
everyone looking for love,
everyone needing to eat.

Bring your morsel here to share;
make the table more complete.
Bring your shame, all your regret:
over now, now take your seat.
Stars are kindling lamps on high,
hearts are filling up with song;
let it cradle all your pain,
even scars will sing along.

Life's old Story in the flesh,
tell its chapters here by heart;
some so painful, some so sweet,
mystery hid in every part.
Laugh like children at surprise,
cry the tears that make things new:
everywhere it tells of me,
everywhere it tells of you.

Bread is Heaven's kindest dream;
Wine, its deep spellbinding kiss.
Filled with so much more than food:
nothing's better, Lord, than this.

Maybe we can even love,
call off battles and forgive;
peaceful, peaceful to abide,
eat, and drink, and fully live.

Suggested use as part of a confession and assurance or as an invitation to the table. Because the tune may be unfamiliar, it might be best arranged for choir or sung by a soloist, or by choir or soloist alternating with the congregation.

We Need to Eat

VINCE AMLIN

INVITATION

Psalm 23 says,
"You prepare a table before me
in the presence of my enemies."
Maybe that's so I can gloat over the feast self-righteously.
Smack my lips. Lick my fingers.
Make a show of how delicious it is
to have the Lord as my Shepherd.
Maybe.

Or maybe it's because the Good Shepherd knows
that when my enemies and I are less hangry,
when our cups are full
and we can't get more than a table's-width away from one another,
goodness and mercy may follow.

Who stands across from you at this meal?
Whose place-card has God awkwardly arranged in your eye-line?
Who hungers for your forgiveness?
Whose mercy do you crave?
God has spread this table of love for you.
Who will you invite to eat?

PRAISE AND THANKS

The meal is beginning...

God be with you
And also with you.

Lift up your hearts.
We lift them up to God.

Let us give thanks to God.
It is right to give our thanks and praise.
God, you created us with a need to eat.
Gifted us with a hunger and thirst that draw us together,
friend, and stranger, and enemy.
Over a bite of fruit,
or a bowl of pottage,
roasted lamb and unleavened bread,
a day's ration of manna,
or an all-you-can-eat quail buffet,
a honeyed scroll,
a spicy ember,
flour and oil,
loaves and fish,
bread and wine.

REMEMBERING JESUS

We remember that on the last night of his life,
Jesus gathered his disciples
at a table of grace
to show them what was possible.
He took bread, and broke it,
and gave it to the irritating ones,
the false ones, the proud ones,
the tired ones, the wishy-washy ones.
And he told them,
This is my body, broken for you.
When you hunger to get even, remember.

Then he took a cup and gave thanks.
The same cup of which he said
one who shared it would betray him.
And he gave it to them, saying,
This is my blood, poured out for you.
When you thirst for vengeance, remember.

And so we ask,
Holy Spirit, bless these signs of God's unfailing mercy.
And bless the need to eat
that has drawn us into this feast.
As we reach out our arms in blessing,
may our prayers extend
to the friends and strangers who surround us.
And even to the enemies
in whose presence we are fed.
May this meal make a new world possible. Amen.

Eating Danger

MARY LUTI

"Here I am! I stand at the door and knock. If anyone hears my voice and opens the door, I will come in and eat with that person, and they with me." (Revelation 3:20, NRSV)

Jesus was always knocking at other people's doors. Whenever he got invited to a meal, he went. He didn't care who the host was, or who else was on the guest list. But some people disapproved: "He's eating with tax collectors and sinners!"

Jesus' critics were not the first nor last to discourage indiscriminate dining. Not the first nor last to demand obedience to rules of social non-engagement. If you want to keep your own kind safe, pure, and clear about their place in the system, you have to be careful whom you eat with.

Eat with just anyone, and it could be trouble. You might catch their cooties. They might learn your name. They might tell you stories. You might like their stories. You might start wondering what all the fuss is about. And what begins as "Pass the ketchup" becomes "May I have one of your fries?" Before you know it, everybody's making friends, hanging out at the local bar, falling in love, having sex and babies.

There's a reason some of the nastiest violence of the civil rights era was unleashed on people trying to integrate lunch counters.

When Christ says, "I'll eat with you, and you with me," it sounds like a tender pledge. But it's more threat than promise. It's a threat of barrier-breaking intimacy. A threat to share fries and marry outside the family. A threat to sabotage every kind of caste and distinction.

If you eat with him, you might come down with something. Who knows where it will end?

O Christ Who Knocks, We Hesitate

WORDS: **MARY LUTI**
TUNES: **DURROW, MAPLE AVENUE, KINGSFOLD**
8.6.8.6.D

O Christ who knocks, we hesitate
to welcome you inside,
for fear that you might stay too long
and leave nowhere to hide.
Persuade us now to entertain
your Presence that intrudes,
till all the purity we prize
lies scattered and confused.

O Christ who knocks, we hesitate
when you, our danger, call.
Remove our caution and our dread
and help us risk it all.
Free every table fenced with fear,
release what we withhold;
the pain of love and joy denied
in Mercy's arms enfold.

O Christ, our undermining guest,
too close for comfort here;
our threat and saving remedy
for separating fear,
with healing breath infect us now,
your kiss of peace bestow,
and we will live befriending lives,
defenseless, like your own.

Suggested use as a prayer before Communion. May be useful on a racial justice Sunday. See also its use in the creative activity, "Who's at the Door?"

Who's at the Door? Collaboratively Creating Communion

KAJI DOUŠA

Outside of the context of worship, gather some congregants who love a meal. Maybe it's the people who most often find themselves stirring or scrubbing pots. It could be the resident poet. It could be the soul who always remembers to pick up the juice or wine just in time, or the saint who smooths the linens just so. It could be the child who conspires to finish the last morsels of bread after church. Set the invitation wide enough to allow someone to surprise you.

Gather for a meal together, whether in a shared physical space or with the help of the digi-verse. (Holy Spirit has a way of being anywhere, she can handle the trip.) With this assembly of saints, begin with prayer. Invite Jesus, your companion guest and host. Give thanks for the gift of presence, for the bounty and the inspiration. Next, invite your guests to respond to some prompts in writing, with the option to share their responses (as much or as little as they wish) as part of the liturgy to come.

Encourage your guests to write, asking:

1. Who would Jesus call a friend? Make a long, specific list.
2. How far would Jesus go to reach a friend?
3. When has Jesus gone to lengths for you?
4. How has God surprised you?
5. What feels risky in opening yourself up to God?
6. How is God showing up in your community?
7. Can you think of a time when you've experienced the Holy Spirit? How did it feel? How did you know? Describe the encounter.
8. What would you like to thank God for doing?

As you offer these prompts, expect astonishment. Expect resistance, too. Stay with it and notice what cues both.

Now, listen to your people as you share this love feast.

WELCOME

Welcome to God's love feast, where Christ is our host and our guest. Welcome, *[guests share their lists from #1]*.

THANKS

We give thanks that *[guests share their responses from #2]*.

TESTIMONY

We testify to *[guests share their responses to #3]*.
We acknowledge that *[guests share their responses to #4]*.

TRUST

Through all of this, you know, O God, that we approach you with fear and trembling. Silently before you, we lay down these fears on your table: [guests pray on their own responses to #5].

REMEMBERING

Gathering all this and so much more, with praise and thanksgiving we remember: [Tell here the story of Jesus and the meal; bless the bread and cup.]

PRAYER TO THE HOLY SPIRIT

Let us pray: Make your Holy Spirit known to us, O God, in these your bountiful gifts. We give thanks that you continue to show up for us, remembering:[guests share their responses to #6].

PRAYING

[Recite the Lord's Prayer together.]

SHARING THE MEAL

Beloved in Christ, God has promised to show up at this table and is present, right now. We give thanks for ways God has, does, and will show up, remembering them before you now. [Guests share responses to #7.]

And now, we share this blessed meal. *[Eat! Drink! Be thankful!]*

THANKSGIVING

Let us give thanks to the God who always, always shows up for us. Thank you for: *[guests share their responses to #8]*.

After you've finished, encourage everyone to scribe their responses on a huge sheet of paper, a whiteboard, whatever you have to lay it all out in front of you. Marvel in what God has done, collect it all, return to it.

PLEASE, COME IN

Communion, Hospitality and Healing

Let's Not Die Today, Shall We?

MARY LUTI

Later on that same day, two of them were going to a village called Emmaus, about seven miles from Jerusalem, and talking with each other about all these things that had happened. While they were talking and discussing, Jesus himself came near and went with them, but their eyes were kept from recognizing him... As they came near the village, he walked ahead as if he were going on. But they urged him strongly, saying, "Stay with us, because it is almost evening." So he went in to stay with them. When he was at the table with them, he took bread, blessed and broke it, and gave it to them. Then their eyes were opened, and they recognized him, and he vanished from their sight. (Luke 24: 13-16, 28-31, abridged)

These two disciples aren't strolling, they're fleeing. They aren't just disappointed; they're scared to death. The Romans had executed Jesus, his followers could be next. Given the danger, it may surprise us, who are always pondering the next best way to protect ourselves, that they so easily accept this stranger. They even ask him in to eat.

But if you've visited the Middle East, you know it's not that surprising. There's a naturalness to hospitality there, a reflex of readiness to put oneself out for another, even if it's inconvenient, costly, or unwise.

Some say this reflex is historically rooted in the region's geography. In a harsh climate with scant resources, hospitality was a necessity, not a nicety. You never turned anyone away: it could just as easily be you needing water, a decent meal, some company, a story, a bit of shade.

If that's true, hospitality isn't something you offer because you believe the stranger might turn out to be an angel (or Jesus) in disguise. No, it's a matter of survival, an acknowledgement that we're all at the mercy of life's harsh elements, and that if no door is opened to us, no table set for us, no bread offered, no wine poured in the company of others, despair is sure.

The wondrous thing is that sometimes, as on that luminous evening at the table in Emmaus, hospitality ends in recognition, presence, shattering joy. But it begins elsewhere, in a door that opens in the midst of need, in a blessing over shared food and drink, in simple human presence. Without you, I die. Without me, so do you.
Let's not die today, shall we?

Please, come in.

Will Anyone Throw Wide a Door?

WORDS: **MARY LUTI**
TUNE: **SHOUT ON**
8.6.8.7.6.D.

Will anyone throw wide a door,
welcome in a stranger?
Will anyone extend a hand,
never mind the danger?
The path of life is often pain,
shadowed and unknowing.
Will anyone come in the night,
welcome light bestowing?

A table set, a blessing song,
these revive the living.
Will anyone be host and friend,
heaven-sent and giving?
The path of life is often pain:
there our Christ is waiting
with bread beside an open door,
Love unhesitating.

Suggested use as an invitation to the table, an assurance after confession, or a post-Communion song of sending.

This Is the Place, Come In

MARY LUTI

INVITATION

Life is hard.
The path is often full of pain.
We need to know we won't be alone.
We need to know there will be a light in the shadows,
a door open, a table set,
someone to offer us a loaf and a cup,
a song and a story to revive our flagging hearts:
a safe refuge till morning.

Dear friends, you have come to that place.
Here Christ waits for you and welcomes you without question.
So come, let yourself be cared for and fed by our faithful, tender friend.

REMEMBERING

Now let us pray:
We remember, Gracious God, that from the beginning
you desired that we live and not die,
thrive and not wither, find company and not be alone.
You met us in the wilderness with manna,
in the forty-day desert with angels,
in the night of betrayal with a feast.

Whenever we went astray,
you came for us and brought us home.

And you sent us Jesus,
who longed to gather us like a hen safeguards her chicks;
who told us the truth about life and its dangers,
about the man set upon by robbers, left for dead,
and the enemy stranger who cared for him and became his neighbor.

Jesus told us to be neighbors, too:
to have no fear in welcoming and tending,
to be ready at our doors with a light.

We remember that he called us friends
although he knew that we would turn him away
when he needed us most.
On that night when we betrayed him
he gave us bread and wine,
signs of the risk he took for us in his own body,
the life he surrendered in love.

And he promised to be with us
every time we eat this meal together,
so that we would never be afraid
because we are never alone.

PRAYER TO THE HOLY SPIRIT

We ask you, Holy Spirit, to bless this bread and cup,
love made food for our safety and consolation.
As we eat and drink together,
fill us with hope and make us brave.
Keep us, like Christ, beside our doors, holding a light,
saying to every shadowed stranger: Here, right here, come in.

[The Lord's Prayer may be recited here.]

SHARING BREAD AND CUP

THANKSGIVING

Who is like you, Gracious One?
There is no one like you,
our feast and our song,
our safety and our story,
our hope and our peace.
There is no one like you.
Thank you, now and always. Amen.

Come and Have Breakfast

MARY LUTI

The other disciples followed in the boat, towing the net full of fish… When they landed, they saw a fire of burning coals there with fish on it, and some bread. Jesus said to them, "Come and have breakfast." (John 21:8-9 & 12, NIV)

Years ago, a young man began coming alone to worship. He sat in the back and spoke to no one, except the greeters, who never got more than a "Good morning."

He stood and sat as indicated, but the pastor could see even from up front that he couldn't get through the hymns. He'd crumple, sit back down. The pastor wanted to talk to him, but the young man fled before the benediction.

One of the deacons noticed him, too. She began sitting in the pew in front of him. After a while, she sat in his pew. One morning, she passed the peace to him and made serious eye contact. He didn't move away.

She told the pastor it felt like befriending an animal; slow, gentle habituation, like you do with a skittish rescue. She didn't mean it condescendingly; it was a tender observation.

On a Communion Sunday, he didn't stir when it was time to go forward. She whispered to him, "Are you coming?"

"No," he said, "I've done some bad things."

She nodded, waited, then said, "But do you want to come?"

His pain showed. "I can't."

She said, "Well, you'd be welcome."

She went. He stayed. But the following Sunday he asked if there would be Communion. She said no, although if he wanted it she'd ask the pastor if something could be done.

What was said and done next the pastor and deacon weren't free to say. But a few months later, after the young man had moved away, he sent them a note. It started with some verses from John 21 about Peter the denier, and Jesus who'd made breakfast for him.

He thanked the deacon for her gentle invitations. He thanked the pastor for organizing Communion in the parlor for him after church that day. He said he still felt ashamed and unworthy, but grateful, too, because feeling unworthy had made him a magnet for Jesus, or at least for one of Jesus' deacons. He still sits in the back of his church, still crumples at the hymns. But he lets Christ's mercy feed him.

At Sundown on the Feast

WORDS: **MARY LUTI**
TUNES: **CLIFF TOWN (ERIK ROUTLEY), SHELDONIAN**
10.10.10.10

At sundown on the feast you summoned friends
to share the meal of liberating bliss;
and when you washed their feet you bent as well
to one who'd soon betray you with a kiss.

As evening stars appeared, a fleeing pair,
afraid and disenchanted by your doom,
begged you to eat with them, their newfound Friend,
and glimpsed in broken bread the empty tomb.

From shore at dawn you told fainthearted friends
to cast again and find more than enough;
then 'round the breakfast fire your mercy made,
without a shaming word you spoke of love.

Now in this holy circle, tender Christ,
enfold us once again in love's embrace.
O bend before our fragile human need,
and feed our waiting hearts with grace on grace.

Suggested use in Holy Week and Easter as a Communion hymn or during a ritual of confession and assurance on Communion Sundays.

Eating with Jesus

LIZ MILLER

INVITATION

A local diner where the waitress greets you by name.
A cup of hot tea poured by a friend in her cozy kitchen.
A summer camp dining hall buzzing with youthful joy.
A family table where favorite dishes get passed a second and third time.

Shared meals have the power to transform, to heal,
to reorient us toward love.
A shared Communion meal draws us back to God,
to sacred healing, to our place in the Body of Christ.

If you have come to this Communion meal today
craving comfort and peace,
hungering for justice and mercy, thirsting for reconciliation and grace,
the invitation to eat is for you.

Come to the table to break life-giving bread
and linger over a cup of blessing.
Come to the table to remember that you are loved.
We have been saving a seat just for you.

THANKS AND PRAISE

O God who meets us on the lakeshore and at banquet tables,
who huddles around bonfires and in church kitchens,
we give thanks that wherever we gather, you find us.
When we feel lost, you offer us a home in the comfort of your love.

Whether we are strangers or friends, family or neighbors,
help us to feel your grace in the people around this table.
In serving one another, may we live your call to be your servants.
Thank you for the many ways you feed us,

from early morning feasts to late night snacks.
Thank you for the food you offer us for our spirits,
food that nourishes and soothes, food that satisfies and delights.

REMEMBERING JESUS

We remember the supper shared with disciples
the night before Jesus' arrest,
and we remember another meal shared on the road to Emmaus,
the resurrected Christ meeting his disciples in their grief,
hope clouded by despair, hearts poured out in conversation.
As he had done so before, Jesus gave thanks,
he broke the bread and offered it to his friends.
They ate, and instead of grief, they tasted grace.
They drank, and instead of despair, they recognized love in their midst.

PRAYER TO THE HOLY SPIRIT

Holy Spirit, take this bread and cup
and transform them into the bread of life and the cup of blessing.
Prepare our weary hearts to feast on a welcome that includes all.
In eating together, may we be one as the Body of Christ.

INVITATION TO THE TABLE

Let us come to the table and eat,
knowing nothing can keep us separate from Christ's welcome and love.

THANKSGIVING

Thank you for this meal shared in the company of friends.
Having rested and been fed, may we go from this place
committed to feeding any person who hungers for love,
offering the same blessings we have received.

Breakfast at Dawn

MARY LUTI

INVITATION

Dear friends, here at this table the Spirit welcomes us all.
Here she gives special honor to the hungry and poor.
Here she embraces creation with healing and peace.
Here she pledges a graceful age to come, an age of justice and dignity.
Here she lets us perceive it and shows it to the world, a new way of being together—
pardon and healing, service and care, joy in the eating, justice in what we say and do.
So come, eat and drink, receive new life, and rejoice in it, together, as Jesus desired.

THANKS AND PRAISE

Let us pray:
From the first day to the last, O God,
you are generous and kind,
filling the world with mercy's bread,
drenching us with mercy's wine.
You give us gifts too many to count,
our hearts are glad when we remember you.
Even in the midst of death, life abounds.
And so we praise you, singing your goodness and glory
with every creature you made:

SANCTUS

Holy, holy holy.... *[or another short hymn of praise may be used].*

REMEMBERING JESUS

And now, O God, with grateful hearts, we remember Jesus.
When all seems lost, when we are stuck in sadness, stymied by shame,
when nothing we try resurrects our hope,

Christ comes to us with morning light.
He tells us where to cast the nets.

The catch is amazing; our nets are full to breaking.
He knows we are hungry, and he feeds us well.

On shore he lights the breakfast fire
and grills the fish for us, and bread.

Sorrow and guilt fade in the mist of morning.
We eat together, speaking only of love.

It is always this way with him—
food and pardon,
mercy and life,
love and more love.

Even on the night we betrayed him,
he gave us bread and wine,
and asked us to remember him
whenever we gather and share them with thanks.

PRAYER TO THE HOLY SPIRIT

So come, Holy Spirit,
bless this bread and cup,
signs of the Love that meets us on every shore,
at every dawn, after every hard night,
always eager to feed and forgive, to bless and send.
For all who receive these gifts with thanks,
make them food and drink of resilient life,
until your new age of justice comes
and every creature beholds it.
In Jesus' name we pray. Amen.

Medicine of Heaven

MARY LUTI

Then Jesus said to them, "Very truly, I tell you … the bread of God is that which comes down from heaven and gives life to the world… Whoever eats of this bread will live forever." (John 6:32-33 & 51, NRSV)

Many early Christians thought Jesus was talking about Communion here. Of course, at this point Jesus didn't know what Communion was—he hadn't given us that gift yet. But our forebears heard that meaning in Jesus' words anyway.

They'd come to experience the presence of Christ with them in Communion as life-giving, and they spoke of Communion as medicine for what ails us. They believed that partaking of the bread and wine shored up and mended their frail human condition. To approach Communion was to be diagnosed, admitted, treated, and released to a new regimen of health and resilience, body, mind, and soul.

Regularly partaking also vaccinated you against the estrangement that destroys human solidarity. Being in communion with the Healer and all our convalescing siblings in the church staved off deadly infections like a divided heart, moral indifference, and an evasive life.

Communion was also a foretaste of the permanent health of the life to come. Exactly what such a fully wholesome life would be like, no one knew, but it had to be at least something like Communion— the beloved as one in the Beloved, feasting.

But the most important thing was how you knew the medicine was taking. The proof lay in service. The church's body was healing when it found itself caring about and tending bodies, defending people against injury and violence, dehumanization and contempt. It could claim health only when it was putting its own body on the line.

Which is why examining the life we lead in our bodies has traditionally preceded Communion. It's a wellness check, and if it shows we've been indifferent or hostile to our neighbors' bodies, we know we need to come to the table again, and again, to eat the Bread that heals us, then go and do otherwise.

Bread of Life from Heaven's Hand

WORDS: **MARY LUTI**
TUNES: **JESU KREUZ LEIDEN UND PEIN, AVE VIRGO VIRGINUM**
7.6.7.6.D

Bread of life from heaven's hand,
nurse our pain and sorrow.
Pardon for our aching past,
healing for tomorrow.
Bread of Life from heaven's hand,
brace our weak condition.
Keep us safe from sin and harm,
merciful physician.

Bread of Life from heaven's hand,
fill our friendless longing.
Seat us at your table home,
feed us with belonging.
Bread of Life from heaven's hand,
end of all our fasting;
life as it was meant to be:
wholeness everlasting.

Bread of Life from heaven's hand,
in the body find us.
Towel and basin at our feet,
neighbor love, entwine us.
Bread of Life from heaven's hand,
bond of flesh revealing
countless wounds to kiss and mend
with you, Jesus, kneeling.

Suggested use for healing services when Communion is also being served; also for a foot washing service.

Remedy and Balm

QUINN CALDWELL

We remember what you told us to become:

Healers and justice-makers,
prayers and creators,
lovers and helpers,
blessers and blessings,
repenters and second-chancers,
givers and forgivers,
spiritual and earthy.

We remember that you told us to be
salt and light,
children new-born and reborn.

And we remember in silence
the unique becoming you willed
for each of us alone:

[Silence is kept.]

We have not finished our becoming.
We are not yet what you hoped.

So here we are, with hands opened
and throats dried.
Here we are for filling,
and quenching, and becoming.

With all your people
down through the ages,
who approach you hoping to be made better
we say:

Give us this bread.
Tell us you have saved the best vintage for now.

Once, you told a room full of
not-yet-finished believers and
unbecoming becomers
that you, you yourself
were the healing they didn't know they needed.
Once, you blessed, and broke,
and shared, and sent yourself in their midst.
Renew that work now, for us.

And do not leave us without the consolation
of a Spirit more powerful than our own
to turn this bread to remedy
this drink to balm
this prayer to antidote
and this people to vaccine
against the evil that stalks the world.

[The bread and cup are shared.]

Let this remembering, and sharing,
and proclaiming, and feeding
be the way we become
healers and justice-makers,
prayers and creators,
lovers and helpers,
blessers and blessings,
repenters and second-chancers,
givers and forgivers,
spiritual and earthy,
salt and light,
and childlike,
and new-born.

And if, after a time,
it turns out that we still aren't

quite what you hoped
just yet
then bring us back again
and again
until we are.
Amen.

FOR AS LONG AS IT TAKES

Communion and Perseverance

Devoted

MARY LUTI

They devoted themselves to the teaching of the apostles and to the communal life, to the breaking of the bread and to the prayers. (Acts 2:42, NABRE)

Liturgical scholar James White once called congregational worship "a stubborn communal leaning towards God." We just hang in, week after week. And this persistence—this devotion, this habit—is one of worship's most important, if vastly underrated, contributions to justice-making.

Our need to worship is recurring, just as the struggle against injustice is recurring. By devoting ourselves to worship time and again, we learn the persevering character of that struggle. We practice the doggedness that God eternally brings to the divine mission, so that whenever and wherever Love makes demands, the chances are better we'll show up too, and do what justice requires.

I often think of White's definition in discussions about how often we should celebrate Communion. A common argument against doing it frequently it is that it's "special." Do it too often and it will become mere routine. But there's nothing mere about routine. Routine and repetition are the stuff of growth and depth. We can't become good at anything without them. And God has called the church to become very good at persisting towards justice.

Maybe showing up repeatedly to the table would make us more able to show up to the fray, and to keep showing up in this hard world where injustice is not occasional, but tenaciously routine.

To become doggedly devoted to justice, maybe we don't need "special" and "rare" as much as we need "ordinary" and "available"—frequent chances to enact and practice the devoted resilient perseverance of Jesus, who shows up without fail every time we gather to remember and give thanks.

Good Jesus, Long Ago You Said

WORDS: **MARY LUTI**
TUNES: **BOURBON, DEUS TUORUM MILITUM (GRENOBLE)**
8.8.8.8

Good Jesus, long ago you said,
Each time you gather to be fed,
I'll make you brave by sharing bread
and resurrect you from the dead.

We trust your promise to be near,
at every Feast of Love appear
to eat and drink away our fear
and give us grace to persevere.

Time and again, from feeding hands
new courage comes and love expands,
so that when justice makes demands,
we'll do whatever love commands.

Remember me, you told your friends.
Persist toward all that love intends.
Return a hundred times, and then
return, return, return again.

Suggested use as an invitation to the table, a post-Communion sending, or at any Communion service when themes of justice-making are being explored.

Prayer at the Table: Holy Routine

MARY LUTI

Jesus, you are present here, in bread and cup,
in the company we are keeping,
in this sharing of faith and lives and food.

In holy communion with the suffering,
in holy communion with the poor,
in holy communion with all who need your bread.

You are present here, not for the first time or the last,
not once in a while, but whenever we gather in your name,
every time we remember you and thank our God for you.
You are for us and with us, among us and in us, diligent in pardon,
unceasing in mercy, tender in feeding, closer than our breath.

As often as we meet here to do this,
by your devoted presence
transform our vacillation into steadiness,
our timidity into courage,
our hesitation into readiness,
our fear into faith.

By your showing up faithfully to eat and drink with us,
make us a Body that shows up for the world every day,
taking up where we left off the day before,
beginning at the beginning we never leave behind.

Teach us the wisdom of routine,
like practicing scales and filling sketchbooks.
Keep us dividing loaves, pouring cups,
blessing and thanking, giving and receiving,
until we acquire the habit of mercy,
the reflex of justice, the routine of making peace.

For this world's evil is routine,
it is recurring and tenacious.
The enemies of love practice every day,
rehearsing havoc to perfect it.
They don't rest.
Make us tenacious too, practicing the craft of love,
learning it at your table,
all in, and devoted, Christ, to you.

How Often? Until

MARY LUTI

For as often as you eat this bread and drink the cup, you proclaim the Lord's death until he comes. (1 Corinthians 11:26, NRSV)

Some congregations have Communion once a month. Others do it quarterly. And some celebrate the sacrament weekly, which is what I advocate whenever I'm debating this subject. I can give you a hundred reasons why I'm right. But I won't. Because the truth is that you can make all kinds of good arguments for other intervals, too.

For Paul and the Corinthians, weekly was probably the norm. But it wasn't the point. Paul was more interested in meaning than intervals. He told the church that by eating and drinking, they were keeping the dangerous memory of Jesus alive in the world while they awaited his return. For our Christian forebears, the answer to "how often?" wasn't weekly or monthly. It was until.

How often should Communion be celebrated?

Until the poor you now exclude from life's feast have pride of place at the Banquet.

Until no one is poor.

Until the food you bless and share only among yourselves is food blessed and shared with all the hungry.

Until no one is hungry.

Until the unjust deaths you so casually forget are remembered, and every victim resurrected.

Until there are no more unjust deaths.

Until the New Age of justice and love you now work against every time you deny mercy to the sinner, liberation to the oppressed, love to the despised, and joy to the sorrowful fully occupies your heart.

Until that New Age comes.

How often should we celebrate Communion?

As often as it takes.

Until Christ comes.

And Now We Eat Together

WORDS: **MARY LUTI**
TUNES: **WEDLOCK (LOVELACE), HEAVENLY ARMOUR (WILLIAM WALKER)**
7.6.7.6.D

And now we eat together
while waiting for the Day.
And now we drink together
while working for the Day.
And now we hope together
while Justice makes a Way,
returning to this table
'till Heaven comes to stay.

And now, good Jesus, lead us
and live in us we pray,
be food and daily courage
along the Mercy Way.
And we will keep on loving
no matter what they say,
today and still tomorrow,
'til Heaven comes to stay.

Suggested use as a hymn that wraps around the Communion liturgy, with the first verse serving as an invitation to the table and the second verse as a post-Communion sending.

Is It Time Yet?

PHIWA LANGENI

Is it time yet?
It is time, yet we routinely exclude people from receiving God's abundant goodness at the table and elsewhere.

Is it time yet?
It is time, yet we zealously cling to the ways we've always done things to mute our fears of change.

Is it time yet?
It is time, yet we narrow-mindedly reject new perspectives that challenge our own.

Is it time yet?
It is time, yet we carelessly stunt the growth that God would have us experience from unexpected places and people.

Is it time yet?
It is time, yet we thoughtlessly blame the oppressed for the various violences done against them.

Is it time yet?
It is time, yet we arrogantly perform our activism to increase our social currency and credibility.

Is it time yet?
It is time, yet we falsely believe in the illusions of control and independence.

Is it time yet?
It is time, yet we willfully choose ignorance at the cost of the lives and wellbeing of so many across the globe.

Is it time yet?
It is time, yet we hypocritically preach God's radical justice that we do not practice.

Is it time yet?
It is time, yet we recklessly shirk our responsibilities to God's diverse creation for the sake of convenience.

[Observe a brief silence here.]

Is it time yet?
It is time, yes! It is time to unselfishly receive God's transcending love to guide our living and relating.

Is it time yet?
It is time, yes! It is time to undeservingly accept God's transforming grace for our imperfect efforts of doing and being the Church.

Is it time yet?
It is time, yes! It is time to unswervingly perceive God's transfiguring presence in and all around us.

Is it time yet?
It is time, yes, it is time! Thanks be to God!

Not Done Yet

MARY LUTI

"But God raised him on the third day and allowed him to appear... to us who were chosen as witnesses, and who ate and drank with him after he rose from the dead." (Acts 10:40-41, NRSV)

The Last Supper wasn't. Jesus ate a bunch of meals with his friends after that "last" one. A snack of fish in a locked room, breakfast on a beach, supper in Emmaus, and untold other meals shared in the forty days before he ascended.

Dying and rising didn't affect his appetite. With all that eating it's as if he's saying, "The worst thing happened. But look at us now. Me, with scars in my shining flesh; you, with new courage in your timid hearts. We made it. We're not done yet. We live to feast another day!"

It's the story of our lives, and the story of the church. The worst things happen. They do awful damage. Yet, somehow, we're back, weary and scarred, but breathing, more or less upright, taking nourishment at the table of grace. We're not done yet. Not done blessing, serving, singing, giving thanks. Not done washing feet, feeding, consoling, emptying jails. Not done multiplying justice like bread. Not done feasting with Jesus at the table of joy.

Which makes me wonder: instead of always doing Communion as a Last Supper of broken body and poured out blood, why don't we eat more Suppers of Resilient Awe together, more Snacks in the Locked Room, more Breakfasts on the Shore, more Dinners in Emmaus, more astonished Feasts of the Forty Days?

The words of institution at those Communion meals might go something like this: "The worst happened. But here we are, and so are you. OMG, we're not done yet. Pass the bread, good Jesus; pour the wine!"

But We Got Up

WORDS: **MARY LUTI**
TUNES: **THE TURTLE DOVE, TRURO, JERUSALEM (WILLIAM WALKER), TALLIS' CANON**
8.8.8.8

O pass the bread and pour the cup!
The worst befell, but we got up!
Remember always, don't forget!
Let's eat and drink, we're not done yet!

Suggested use as a meditation sung repeatedly before and/or during the distribution of Communion. It could also be used as an invitation to the table.

Resilient

MARY LUTI

PRAISE, THANKS, AND REMEMBERING

O God, we remember: the worst thing possible happened to Jesus.
His friends betrayed and abandoned him.
The Romans tortured and killed him.
His traumatized disciples hid and fled.

But some women went to the tomb.
They came back announcing he'd been raised from the dead.
Then it started happening to the rest:
some in a locked room, some on the lake in Galilee,
some on the road to Emmaus.

They saw him, touched his wounded flesh.
He asked them, "Children, is there anything to eat?"

And so they ate with him again—meals of wonder, meals of joy,
trembling meals of healing for all they'd been through,
simple meals of nourishment for all that lay ahead.
Meals like this one, O God, at this table, here and now.

The Spirit has called us, and we've come,
with scars and traumas, failings and fallings,
to find Jesus here, and a company of friends,
weakened and wounded, who by grace and grit are not done yet.

We're so grateful for this bread and cup, and for this company.
We ask the Spirit to bless them and us,
as memory makes Christ present in this word of truth:
The worst thing possible happened. It was awful.
But, by God, we're not done yet!

You're still with us, Jesus, eating.
You're still with us, Jesus, resilient.
You're still with us, Jesus, not yet done.
And we are still here, too.
So pass the bread, good Jesus! Pour the wine!

Index of Scripture

Index of Topics

Index of Tunes

About the Contributors

MARY LUTI is a long-time seminary educator and the author of *Teresa of Avila's Way* and numerous articles on the practice of the Christian life.

KENNETH L. SAMUEL is Pastor of Victory for the World Church (UCC) in Stone Mountain, Georgia. He is the author of *Solomon's Success: Four Essential Keys to Leadership*.

KAJI DOUŠA is Senior Minister of The Park Avenue Christian Church in New York City.

DONNA SCHAPER works nationally for Bricks and Mortals, a NYC-based organization that provides sustainable solutions for sacred sites. Her most recent book is *Remove the Pews*.

LIZ MILLER serves as the pastor of Edgewood United Church (UCC) in East Lansing, Michigan.

JODI HITZHUSEN (professionally, Jodi Heights) is a classically trained soprano, pianist, singer-songwriter, and teacher based in Boston, Massachusetts.

MOLLY PHINNEY BASKETTE pastors at First Church Berkeley (CA) United Church of Christ. She is the author of several books about church renewal, parenting & faith, and spirituality.

MATT LANEY is a United Church of Christ minister and the author of *Pride Wars*, a fantasy series for young readers.

VINCE AMLIN is Co-Pastor of Bethany United Church of Christ in Chicago and co-planter of Gilead Chicago.

CHRIS MERESCHUK is an Unsettled Pastor in the Southern New England Conference with a call to transitional ministry.

QUINN G. CALDWELL is Chaplain of the Protestant Cooperative Ministry at Cornell University. He is the author of *All I Really Want: Readings for a Modern Christmas*.

MARILYN PAGÁN-BANKS serves as Pastor of San Lucas UCC, Executive Director of A Just Harvest, and Adjunct Professor at McCormick Theological Seminary in Chicago.

RACHEL HACKENBERG serves on the national staff for the United Church of Christ. She is the author of the popular Lenten book, *Writing to God*, among other titles.

PHIWA LANGENI is the Ambassador for Innovation & Engagement of the United Church of Christ. They are also Founder of Salus Center, the only LGBTQ resource and community center in Lansing, MI.